The Suicide Notes

Duncan Campbell

To my younger self.
If only you had known; adversity grows beauty, like a
flower in shit.

Part I

Part II

Part III

PART I

Get up.

Why?

Because this is only temporary.

It didn't go the way it was supposed to.

It never does. You'll realise that soon. You just have to ride it out. Sink through the thick oily mass until you break through into the clear, refreshing waters. Now, get up.

GOLDEN MOMENT

*Sitting here in the dark, bathed in the ghostly blue, once
again combing through the words once spoken in hushed
excitement, with the sense of having lost, despite
knowing I never had.*

*I journey through each paragraph in a shameful attempt
to be transported to that time forever frozen in a tragic
beauty, like a butterfly pinned down in a glass case.*

*To burn these pages from existence would be to break
my chains although I fear that regret may walk hand in
hand with my freedom.*

*I am overrun by the forces of my apprehension and will
remain dominated by the melancholy joy of my past.*

*I am a willing prisoner then, trapped in my nostalgia of
a golden era.*

*The perfect torture, as that happy time drifts further
into my history, the present day becomes increasingly
blank and dull as the vibrant artistry of my existence is
slowly washed away leaving my soul, the blank canvas,
in the gallery of life.*

*Then this time, is the chronological tomb of my
splendour, to be visited by the spectre I feel myself
becoming in solemn remembrance of my days in colour.*

Force yourself out of the crumpled mess of takeaway stains and beer sweat, throwing the duvet to the side. No need to make the bed. Perch on the edge of the mountainous heap of springs in yesterday's t shirt and boxers.

The remnants of stuffing are spread thin inside the mattress. Ghosts of comfort, killed by the endless stream of bright-eyed bodies, each taking their turn to slowly sink under the weight of this small room- the same as next door and the one next to that.

Blink around the 2D magnolia box, walls thick with gloss to hide the blemishes. Pull out the carpet, put some bars on the window and you've got yourself a prison cell.

Except, it's not burly guards patrolling the hallways that keep you trapped here. It's the awkward exchanges in the hallway, names you should know by now but struggle to recall.

A dusty shaft of light breaks through the faded nylon curtain, reminding you that the day is in full swing but, yet again, you're hiding from it. The muted but frustrating hum of voices forces itself through the window. Pockets of animated chatter between burgeoning friends are another cruel reminder of the life you were promised.

There's a version of you outside that window somewhere. Deep in a branching reality, there's a version of you that found what you expected.

That person bounces around like a pinball, clattering from conversation to conversation. Sharing laughs and forming bonds. Perfectly lining up with the flipper and being launched full speed towards that shiny hole with flashing lights all around it. The ultimate goal - a direct hit.

The scoreboard clangs and clatters as the points keep rolling up. With immense speed, they bounce off every bumper on the way back until 'High Score' flashes in pixelated orange for the whole world to see. But that person doesn't exist.

Instead, you rattled out of the pocket with the full weight of the spring behind you. Everything had been building to that moment as the potential energy grew, ready to be unleashed. But as soon as the coil released, the momentum died. You missed every bumper on the way down and slipped straight through the gap. Zero points.

A stack of books sits on the desk, unread and taunting you. There's nothing interesting inside. But you know that, at some point, you'll have to comb through them, picking out enough smart sounding quotes to give the impression that you've read and understood it all. Not today though, the bare minimum is still too much.

If you really need to, you can write an essay in a night. You just wish you'd picked something you were interested in. Or at least something you could understand.

Uni isn't about that though- it's about the experience, the invaluable lessons, the lifelong friendships. At least, that's what people say.

And maybe you have learnt something about life- That it's a con. A mess of expectations and second-hand ambitions force you through the grinder until you're a non-descript functioning member of society. No fulfilment required.

****

This is your routine. Every morning, force yourself up and sit on the edge of your bed, curled inward, staring at the bare carpets. Time slips away as you dissect the world and squash the pieces like a morbidly curious child pulling the legs off insects.

Some days you gather enough energy to make it into Uni for a lecture or the odd seminar, thinking the whole time that today is the day I turn this all around. But it's Saturday.

And besides, they all end the same way- Alone, staring at the darkness and waiting for something new to happen.

It's been like this for months now.

For the first few weeks, you drifted through the hallways, dipping in and out of identical rooms- desperate for a thread to pull you in with the others.

You realised quickly that everybody hides behind the armour of their eccentricities, cautiously revealing flashes of their authentic self in the hope that they will be accepted.

Friendships form quickly and groups emerge, and even if they don't last, they're enough to help people stumble through the first year, hands stretched out in front of them in the darkness. But you haven't found a place anywhere.

You desperately don't want university to be about the experience because the experience is miserable.

Sitting in your boxers, you wonder whether it's too late now. The walls are up and there is no way for you to forge a real connection with anybody. And at this point, you aren't even sure you want to.

Back home, things were so easy. Your young adult self-inherited the friends you made by accident as a kid. They moulded your identity and you grew naturally as a pack, none of you ever having to make a definitive decision about who you were.

Now, it's up to you to work out who you want to be. The problem is you don't have an answer. You've been cut loose on a life raft with empty advice and everybody else's idea of your direction. They told you the open space would be liberating but it's terrifying.

****

You shuffle over to the door. Footsteps and weary half greetings drift through the gap as hungover bodies drag themselves awake.

Listen for a while until it falls silent. Pull the weighty door, grabbing a damp towel from the back of the busted office chair on your way out.

The scalding water burns some semblance of feeling into you, if only for a moment. Cocoon yourself in it, close your eyes and picture a simpler time, when everything was building towards that first step- the springboard to endless possibilities.

You were confident, certain you'd dive into the world and make it. Instead, you slipped and tumbled into the frozen void. The stream of water dips in pressure, spitting an icy spray over your body.

For a moment, you feel something else.

As you get out of the shower, the clean feeling gives you a burst of energy. You're still beige, but there's a spark of something in there. A glimmer of hope that you can turn things around. Get on a positive track. Take the first step, starting with that essay.

Stride back into your room with renewed purpose and throw your curtains open. Vitamin D and fresh air. Healthy choices. Creeping doubt. Drink more water, eat an orange.

Open the books. You're already making progress, but it's hard to care. Hit the keys with heavy fingers. Read it back. How fucking boring.

Just get the words down, you'll feel better afterwards. Who cares if it's bad? Who cares if it gets done in the first place? Who cares?

Shut the laptop. Stand up and pace around the room. Slap yourself in the face. Get out for a walk.

****

The park is sweltering. Crowds of people mill about in the midday haze, dodging around as you sit on a bench, watching the breeze. The sun and the calm of the greenery dampens the constant feeling of dread, leaving you floating in an empty space.

Memories of your adolescence drift in and out. The confidence of feeling like you knew everything, without any of

10

the anxieties and pressure of the adult world, is a peaceful place to be. A life filled with opportunity and possibility, not hurdles and indecisiveness.

Open your phone and scroll through the list of names, finger hovering above the call icon. Just give in and catch up with one of them. It'll make you feel better.

You decide against it, convincing yourself that they've all moved on to better things. It's just you that fell through the cracks while everybody else is thriving.

Flick through old photos instead, half smiling to yourself as you recapture that feeling of aimless direction. The long nights, underage in the beer garden of the King's Arms. Faces you never speak to anymore, captured with arms around each other.

You tell yourself you've stumbled across the name of an old girlfriend, but you were searching for it. You read through the texts, relishing in the amazing naivety of first loves. The sheer intensity of emotion would be scary to you right now, but when you've never felt the other side of it, you're just running on a high.

The ease of it all perfectly encapsulates that moment in your life. Getting back there would let you shed the dead skin that is dragging you down and emerge fresh.

Except, the beauty of first loves is always soured by the memory of first heartaches. Maybe it's all a lie too. This nostalgia you're feeling is just rose-tinted glasses, desperate measures to find a way out of the tumbling avalanche of apathy.

You want to push forward, but it's been so long you can't help but wonder if it's all too late.

****

The sun begins to dip and the crowds filter out of the park. You watch the swirl of pinks and oranges drag through the cloud as the sun sets and the evening creeps ever closer, pushing students from the grass and back to their kitchens. You can feel the anticipation of the night beginning to swell as you catch snippets of conversation from passing groups.

"Where we off tonight?"
"Nah, not there, it's shit."
"Who cares, it's cheap."

While everybody else is out making memories, you'll be in your cell, unblinking and alone. A night to punish yourself with a million reasons why you can't be out there with them.

But the self-pity is starting to wear thin. Because it's easy really. Just stumble through the mess of social interactions, pour cheap shots down your neck and forget about everything else.

It's more important than the books on your desk, and the half-baked thoughts regurgitated onto the page.

You're getting pissed off, quietly seething on the bench. Tell yourself that you're overreacting, that you're letting yourself down. You write your own story, so stop writing such a shit one.

Get up from the bench and drift behind a group who live upstairs from you, laughing and chatting their way back. You half recognise one of the guys, but not enough to cut into the group uninvited. You've spoken a couple of times outside lectures, maybe if you catch his eye you might be able to fall in seamlessly.

It's only a short jump from walking home to popping in for a beer. From there, it's only natural that you'll go out with them and once you knock down the walls with shit club music and lager poured through cheap lines, the hard part is done.

Laughs about the dumb mistakes of the night before will turn into real conversations. People you drink with become people you talk to sober. But none of it happens without the first step.

Speed up a bit and cut onto the grass to get around them. As you pass, look back and catch his eye. He sees you and gives you a nod, but that's not enough. Give him one back and carry on.

Shit, you're ahead of them now, he's already forgotten you. It was a good effort. Head back to your room, at least you can try get this essay done now.

****

Your heavy eyes drift over the pages, scanning for keywords and phrases. Draw something out, hammer a few lines and get back to the books. It's starting to take shape as a collage of half coherent ideas, cherry picked from a bunch of books by people that know what they're talking about.

If somebody asked you to explain it, you'd choke up and stammer until you could reach into the depths of your memory and regurgitate something you heard somebody else say. But when you have the time to put it down on paper, it's easy to pass off somebody else's ideas as your own.

You're getting good at this now. Every call with friends and family follows the same process as your essay writing.

Grab a few snippets of the things you think you should say and build a picture of a well-adjusted, happy person enjoying the best years of his life.

Yeah, they're all really nice
Been having a great laugh
The course is really interesting

Every time you ignore a call, you just tell them that you had a deadline or you were out with mates. You're simply having too much of a great time to talk to them.

But the truth is, the lies get easier every time and that scares you. You wish you weren't so good at it. If you weren't, they'd force you to talk. But you're an expert at faking it, and that means you're going it alone.

It's probably for the best anyway, you wouldn't want to burden them. The weight of their disappointment when they found out you had failed would be worse than anything that you feel right now.

Your mind is wandering again, you need to focus in on the screen. The flashing cursor mocks you as it stays where it's been sat for the last half an hour. The rumble of the night is beginning to grow in the room a couple doors down the hall.

You hear the distant clang of bottles in carrier bags and the click of heels outside as people converge on rooms, ready to save themselves a bit of cash by necking the cheapest offers from the off license.

The heavy thud of music kicks the door of a room downstairs. Cheers run down the hallway as new people enter and it's decided that the life and soul is here, so things can really begin.

Tribal chants and booze filled rituals accelerate the festivities while you sit there, fingers glued to the keyboard. Just block it out and force some words down. The deadline is creeping up and you're still no closer to reaching it.

Shut the laptop and grab your phone. Go back to those old texts from an ex. Start from the beginning. The cautious messages while you try to test the waters and figure out whether it's worth shooting your shot. The excessively long conversations into the night, rambling about anything and everything so you can avoid severing that connection. You see it in the way that you write.

Then comes the arguments - the I'm Sorrys - the silence.

But a lost relationship won't get you anywhere now. You should just delete them. Cast them into the fire and cleanse yourself, ready to move forward.

But this may be the last sliver of genuine happiness that you'll ever have. If a digital reminder is the best that you'll ever get, isn't that enough reason to keep them?

Put the phone down. You don't have to decide right now, but you do have to get out of this room.

The music has been going on for an hour now, the voices growing louder. At the rate people drink, they'll be fully immersed in a receptive haze, ready to welcome anybody that's here for a good time. The awkwardness will be long gone. Just throw yourself into the midst of it and let them carry you out of this. The essay will get finished eventually. Or it won't, but what do you care?

There are a couple of warm cans left in the ripped open crate under the bed. Power through one and open the next. Finish it on the way to the shop. Pick up another box and head back.

As you turn into your block, a girl that lives a few doors down spills out in search of a drink and instead finds you. She nods at the crate under your arm.

"Hey! Where are you headed tonight?"

Lie. Tell her you're not sure yet. You'll see where the night takes you. The novelty of seeing you engage with people excites her.

"Oh, come out with us!"

It's like a badge of honour for them. They're the ones that got that guy to come out. You'll be their little pet project to show off, before being left at the edge of a dancefloor, nervously sipping from two drinks and going home alone.

Another guy you've seen around here from time to time pokes his head out the door, catches your eye and smiles.

"Wahey. Look who's coming out."

He laughs and slinks back inside the room. Hell, they could be nice. You might become mates if you just drop your guard a bit.

You tell her that you're up for it. She smiles and turns, stumbling a little as she goes into the kitchen.

Stop for a second and take it all in. Close your eyes and listen to the animated voices and repetitive music. Just step inside and leave everything else behind you. Be reborn into the night and wake up with a heavy head and a shared feeling of regret that nobody can take away from you.

"Are you coming in or what mate?"

He pokes his head around the door again and laughs, it's all in good fun. Smile back at him and hoist the crate onto your shoulder. March inside, across the threshold in search of a better version of yourself.

HAVING FUN

Chemical blonde and drowned in an array of pastes and potions crashing through the crowd she comes to me.

I cling to my drink and hug the bar in a drastic attempt to avoid the mahogany harpy swerving, dropping and colliding her way through the zombies, all after one more smack as if it would turn this strobe-lit gulag of hormones into the paradise imagined through the week.

A painted hand wraps around my arm and breaks my dreams of banter and non-adhesive floors.

I turn to gaze upon the colour-palette faced female miming the motion of drinking, my hand ventures into my pocket, the chance this woman will leave post-libation, the perfect motivation to give more money to the barman dancing from beer tap to spirits to waiting notes.

I gesture to the barman with my note in hand – as if coaxing an animal with food – he pirouettes around towards me with the parasitic girl still firmly wrapped around my arm, holding it hostage. I lean over and yell out for two shots of Jack, a glance back at the pile of product beside me and I make mine a double.

Our overpriced drinks arrive, and I slam the tiny glass to my lips in the hope the grim elixir will be down my throat before I have to endure the taste. The woman satisfied, dives for my face, I jerk my head round and avoid a direct assault to the lips and suffer a peck to the neck leaving a red smudge, a badge of my encounter with the boozed-up banshee.

She mimics a jig and asks me to the battleground, and
pouts like a child in response to my refusal, she tugs on
my hand still pleading to continue the unfortunate
encounter. I say I will follow, and she flashes a clown red
grin, spins on her heels and moves to the shuffling mass
vibrating to the bass. I duck back shouldering my
advance to the exit and my freedom.

In a flash I'm out in the air, cool oxygen meets me like
an old friend long missed. I can still feel the thumping
music echoing from the doors. I turn and step over a
frozen figure slumped on the curb and stride off into the
night.

Once again I promise never to endure a club.

Having fun is easy. Children do it every day. Adults try to do it, and when it all goes wrong, just pretend. People find enjoyment in exercise, some people in watching TV. But you'd be hard pressed to find those people tonight.

The chaos of a club pulses through the walls behind you, swallowing more and more bodies into the dark void. Sweat drips down your face as you stop by the cloakroom and exit out the front.

When did nights out stop being fun and instead become some twisted procedural, deemed unsuccessful unless you lose all sense of who you are? Every drink is forced down with such urgency in the hope that it's the one that finally makes the noise stop. But no matter how hard you try, it never does.

Out in the cool breeze of the night with the music rippling behind you, you half whisper to yourself

Never again

Work your arms through the sleeves of your red Harrington and turn the collar up. The lining sticks to the sweat soaking through your shirt, making it feel tighter than usual. Bury your hands in the pockets as a stiff breeze settles on exposed skin. It freezes and evaporates. Goosebumps run down your spine. You smell her perfume and wince.

Walk past the voices queueing from the door and around the corner of the street. Bouncers decked in black puffers and neon armbands stalk the line of half-naked bodies, their eyes glossing over bare legs in short skirts.

"ID'S READY PLEASE!"

You zip your coat and turn your back on the cattle being led to a musical slaughter. Shake your head and repeat the great lie to yourself.

Never again

Damp jeans cling to your thighs, each step chaffing the skin and nipping at your ball sack. You stop for a second to adjust your pants and free yourself from the denim fold.

A glass smashes somewhere in the queue. A bouncer rushes from the door to the scene, flexed arms ready to chuck some dickhead from the line.

"RIGHT, YOU'RE GONE."
"That wasn't even me pal!"
"DON'T GIVE A SHIT. MOVE ON."

One of them swings for the other. Don't turn to look, keep your head down and make for the main street, away from the clash of bodies wrestling down the line.

You stop at the corner where the road turns into the main street of bars and takeaways. A taxi swings to the curb in front of you. Catch your reflection staring at the mess of limbs inside. The door slides open and a group of baby-faced first years clamber out.

Two scrawny lads with black band t-shirts lift their lanky mate out the back seat. His greasy black hair flips with each revolution of his pissed head.

Too much way to early. The only thing carrying him now is the collective view of the group that while he might be down, he's never out.

The taxi driver shakes his head at them and drums his finger on the wheel. You both watch as they prop his body against a wall. The girls of the group wander off to the back of the line.

"Wait up!"
"Take him home, no chance he's getting in."
"Nah c'mon, he'll be fine in a minute."

The driver's automatic door slides shut, he lets on to you with a nod and swerves back into the road and through the night, in search of the next sorry sight with a crumpled twenty in their pocket.

You stand on the edge of the curb, letting your toes hang over and bend toward the street. A voice in your head debates a taxi home. Your empty wallet answers No Chance.

Fuck's sake.

Could always get an Uber, but half the fucking city probably have the same idea right now. You decide to unload the handful of shrapnel in your pocket on the bus and your man in the takeaway.

Cross the road, take the first right onto the main strip where a kaleidoscope of Friday night punters stumble out of bars and into taxis

You feel almost out of breath after the club, the mix of beer and whiskey still burning your throat.

You forgot your headphones which means no music to get you home, just your thoughts and the long path through town.

Wafts of smoke cloud the first bar you pass. Pockets of bodies huddle in their groups, handing out cigarettes and screaming about who's on afters. A lone blonde escapes her gang and wanders barefoot between the gatherings.

"S'cuse me.
Have you got a light?"

Some heavy lad reaches a light from his back pocket. Her drunk fingers try to snap the flame, heels dangling from her other hand. Eventually she gets it going. Like a lost child she wanders back towards you, leaving the guy to chase her down.

"Oi Love. That's my light."

He runs past you and taps her on the shoulder. As she swings around, his face lights up.

She's drunk, he's a chancer. Oldest story there is.

You leave them behind and walk towards the conveyor belt of taxis. If the bodies outside bars huddle, the people in this line swarm.

You drift in and out of the crowd, winding your way between puffed out chests and puddles of girls on the floor. A group of lads throw their arms around each other, sweat pooling under their polo shirts.

"Mate, you got beer at yours?"
"Drank the lot. "
"You lot, let's get a taxi further down."
"Nah man."
"No chance you're getting Dan back with us."

The lads turn to their pal up against a wall with some blonde in jeans and heels. In the rain of jeers and name calling, the couple pretend not to hear. As you walk by, they kiss.

It's like the street goes silent for a moment. A taxi door opens, the guys step inside. And still the couple lean against the wall, holding each other tight; like if they forget the fact that they barely remember each other's name, there might be something special there after all.

Your bus crashes past, its heavy metal frame shuddering over a speedbump. It sighs and puffs to a stop, further than you can be arsed running. A dozen other students sit inside bathed in sterile white light, all drunk and all heading back to halls. There's always another one, you think as you meander along the strip.

A slick BMW with tinted windows muffles a heavy beat behind closed doors. Stop at the crossing and wait for it to swing round the corner, blow the street in a rev of its engine and grind to a halt behind the bus. His horn rages out in the dark. A drunk voice in the night yells back.

"Wahey! Dickhead."

The wind picks its moment to rush a blast of cold air down the side street. You bury your arms in the tight jacket and brace against it. The green man comes, and you cross.

Keep your eyes on the ground, letting the fading light of each closing bar brush through you. It feels almost warm against the cold street.

Press your arms deeper into your jacket and feel the weight of her perfume fill your mind. It's like she's there with you, following you home, her lips still pressed hot against your neck, her tongue moving against yours.

A flashing takeaway sign sears your heavy Jack Daniel eyes. Burp and taste each moment of the night like a bad memory.

"Must have had four snakebites, I reckon.
   Couple of Vodka.
      Then Mitch bought a round of Jaeger Bombs.
         Dunno about the rest of the night."

You look up and see some fresh-faced lass curled up on the steps of a dark restaurant, her bleached hair dangling inches above the ground. She's not thrown up yet, but it's coming. Her friend stands there, looking bored and texting away. A wall of muscles is crouched next to her, stroking her back and consoling her...

"Nah, I promise you'll be good.
   Just need to get you back home.
      Back home and to bed."

She groans and lets her head roll back. A drizzle of hair clouds her face, and you just about make out mascara running down her cheeks. Her mate keeps her eyes locked on the phone.

"Uber says five minutes.
   See love, five minutes and we'll be on our way."

You figure they must only just be 18. Probably not in Uni like the rest of the strip, locals or something like that. Fresh out of college and...

"The fuck are you looking at?"

Muscles stands up and stubs a finger in your direction. You catch yourself staring and sink your eyes on the footsteps rattling beneath you.

"Nah, come back here. You fucking prick."

The mix of Jack and fear burn your cheeks red. You take each step a little faster and a little longer.

Behind you, his dumb voice still calls out, demanding you come back. Pretend you don't hear but listen close to make sure he's not giving chase. You've never swung for someone before, and you're too fucked to start now.

Or maybe you're just the right level of drunk to have a go. Maybe you should turn and try give it some. The crunch of bone against bone, the searing pain as he hits you back and bursts your nose open and you hit the floor. At least it's a feeling, something tangible to puncture the endless days of nothing. A good kicking could be a reminder that you still exist. Each hit reassuring you that people can see you, you're not just a shell, floating through the world, trying to make some kind of impression.

A rock snaps against the pavement and you snap out of it. Your legs move faster down the street. Best to leave it, keep moving to the bus and hope you never see him again.

After a minute, the blood begins to settle in your gut. You put another street between you and him.

Your empty stomach aches and groans through the litres of booze sloshing around. The fear you would never admit to starts to dissipate, replaced by a dull sensation that trickles from your heart to your head.

Clench and unclench your fists.

Repeat the action.

Repeat his words.

The fuck are you looking at?

I'm looking at you, prick

You imagine the escalation of voices. Chests bulge out and arms tense. One of the girls steps in with a leave it, he's not worth it. Not the super pissed one, but her mate surely. Maybe he listens, probably not. He steps up to your face, leans over you.

He's bigger, but at the end of the day, he's an empty wheelbarrow. His voice can thunder and roar, but that's all. You take a step back, clench your fist and snap for his nose. He collapses and you tower victorious, arms held like a boxer in the ring. The crowds on the street roar and rush you.

A car horn blares. You step back from the curb and the taxi rushes past and on to the next fare.

You feel a fool, your heart crashing at a thousand miles an hour over your imagination. Something like common sense rears its head through the mangle of whiskey thoughts and whispers in your ear.

Who are you kidding?
You know who wins in life...

You try to ignore it. Cross the road and press on through the quiet part of the strip. Keep your head down. Ignore the people that pass by. Your stop is just around the next corner, right opposite the takeaway.

It's not worth fighting. It's not worth trying. You'd never take the punch. You'd never take the taxi. You'd never take anyone back to yours. All you are is...

"Yes boss."

Eyes flicker under the damp blue fluorescents. They sting, ache and sterilise in the light. In the corner, a screen crackles a shit Ibiza Anthem with some lass splashing about the ocean in a bikini. Apart from the two guys across the counter, you're the only one in here.

"What can I get you?"
"Yeah, could I get a uh..."

Ripple the change in your pocket. A few pound coins pass through your fingers, should be enough for a...

"10-inch pepperoni please mate"

Dig out the change and count the coins one by one. Your man leans on the high counter and shouts something to the guy in the back. He dumps the change in the till and stares at the screen.

A group of guys step inside, bringing a waft of cologne that mixes with the lingering grease in the air. Their heavy voices boom over the whir of fryers, pounding music and the street outside. Suddenly, it's like you're back inside the club.

"Yes Boss."
"Can I get a uh..."
"Did you see that lass before?"
"Which one?"
"10-inch Hawaiian."
"Mate, you're not getting pineapples on it..."
"In that last bar."
"Proper going for it with her man."
"Get what I want pal."
"Number 52."
"I went for a piss, right?"
"Some chips as well."
"Get us a bottle of coke mate."
"I come back right, and there she is..."
"Hey boss. Number 52."

He's waving a receipt at you. Take your order and mumble some thanks at him. Laughter ushers you out the door and you stumble to the bus stop.

Under the shelter, a few crumpled bodies inhale the last of their cigarettes. It's easy to tell the students from the normal folk- they tend to be the ones trying hardest to measure the night and commit every mad thing that happened to memory.

Who was the most fun? The most drunk? The one who went longest?

Who pulled and who should have tried harder?

With a long metallic groan, the bus lights up the shelter and wheezes its door open. The students get on first and take a seat downstairs. After a slow shuffle through the doors, you rattle a handful of change down for the driver and swing up the narrow stairs.

For the night bus, the top deck is quiet. Properly silent. There's only a handful of folk scattered about. Apart from the couple sat right at the front, the rest of them are alone and look like they're fresh off a long shift. Their feet throb and their backs ache, a long stretch home before doing it all over again tomorrow.

When the bus pulls off, you let yourself relax a little. At least you're moving forward now and don't have to do a thing. Be a half hour to halls and you can space out to the same four walls and ceiling.

Fuck, you've been looking forward to it all night. Ever since she grabbed you, pulled you close and kissed you, you thought...

Can't wait till I'm home

The pizza weighs hot on your lap. You consider a slice but hold off. On a deep inhale you sniff the thick greasy cheese mix with the smell of her perfume, a smell so burnt into you that

27

you can easily pretend not to notice it. But you do, you've smelt it all night and it's haunting.

Try distracting yourself, a drunk plan of action-
Pyjamas. Tea. Laptop. Pizza. Bed.
You honestly can't think of anything better.

The bus jolts over a bump and your eyelids leak open. Shit, did you just dose off?

Come on, you can't be that guy on the bus, letting snores ring out over the top deck, it's sad.

You scan around but everyone else is in their own headphone bubbles.

"What the fuck?"

Your head swivels to the couple at the front. She looks pissed at the guy sat next to her. For the longest minute, their eyes don't break. Something in his face registers what he said and drops his voice to a hushed tone.

She turns and tenses her body from him. The moment for apologies hangs between them. He lays a hand on her shoulder.

"Listen..."
"Are you being serious right now?"
"I just think you're being..."

Cut short with a look.

He draws his hand back and looks out the window at the emptying streets. Something in him goes, like a switch in the mind suddenly clicks.

The sign dings to life.

"You can't even look at me, can you?"

He stands up, his neck crouched under the low ceiling. From where you are sat, it's hard to make out whether he says something as he leaves.

The bus rocks as he thunders down the steps. It pulls in and spits him into the street. She watches him go from above, her head sinking with every step he takes away from her.

Save for the shudder of the bus pulling out, the moment turns into a brittle silence. Laughter filters from the students downstairs and prods at the woman sat alone. She stifles a sob and looks cautiously around, meeting your eyes dead on.

You press the button and take your pizza downstairs. Wherever you are, it's your stop.

Away from the centre of town, the cold air sneaks between the dormant buildings and chills your skin. Your shoulders hunch together, the jacket pulls tight across your back.

Not far now. Just around the next corner then across the small wreck of a park back to your halls. The four floors of bedrooms squat in the skyline, the odd window blinking with late night essays or afters.

Front door in sight, you search inside the jacket pockets, your hand stroking something soft and furry. Pull the jangle of keys out and a small grey teddy holding a heart saying I love you stares back at you.

On another ring there's a picture of two women strapped into a rollercoaster, the speed distorting their cheeks and hair. You think you recognise her face. Drop the keys on the floor and sit on the steps leading up to your door.

Fucking idiot. You know they fine you for that stuff? Grand a month in rent and they find it fair to drop a hundred odd fine on you for a lost key.

Sure enough, someone would be along to let you in. You can't be the only one making your way back. Tonight started with a pint and ended with a pizza, it should be a success story.

In the imposing silence of the building, you force your phone out and start a new note.

Once again, I promise to never endure a club.

You hunch over the pizza box and feel its fading warmth spread across your lap. A dozen more lines spill from your half open eyes and fill the page. You dart and bounce between the lines, starting at the end and filling out passages almost at random.

Put your phone down and flip open the lid of the box in your lap. A Hawaiian pizza stares back at you.

It's honestly enough to make a grown man cry.

TRIALS AND FEAR

*Headphones on, and music full, I shut my eyes, empty
my mind and for the briefest of moments the world is
calm. Float forever in perfect nothingness, a mental
shelter from the avalanche of stress and pressure
bearing down on me with deafening noise and
pyroclastic force.*

*This serenity is severed by the nagging truth that every
moment spent in happiness grates away the joy of those
held most dear.*

*I steady myself to the overwhelming hazard and plunge
into the freezing depths of failure or skip by only to
relive the same in the coming day.*

*My friends and family are the gravity that binds me to
all I wish I could be rid of, for fear of losing memories
and once again, staining the name those before me held
with honour.*

*Should it be that I make it through the academic
abattoir will I see these days to be well spent, or 4 years
of youth dedicated to trials and fear.*

You plug in, left ear then right. Turn on the same playlist,
the same songs. For a minute you sit there, letting the rhythm
settle through your body.

Shut your eyes. Let the pulsing melody calm you, cleansing
your mind of the hell that is about to follow.

It's almost like a ritual. Maybe that's the wrong word, it's
more of a necessity at this point. You've seen those people in
the library, sitting robotically straight with no headphones in.

You wish you had the control, but we both know that level of commitment is beyond you.

Tug your phone out, shuffling through songs in search of something like inspiration. After the string of all-nighters you've pulled, you need anything and everything to see you through this essay.

Six of them this month. A grand total of 12,000 words. 10,000 behind you and 2000 to go. A break for Christmas, then two exams, a presentation then one last essay.

Sigh and shake the thought from your mind. It's easier to not think about the climb when you're at the bottom of the hill. Just put one foot in front of the other.

You knew there'd be work when you started, but honestly you thought you'd be better prepared to take it on. You promised yourself you wouldn't, but you let each workload get left nearer and nearer to the deadlines. So, you end up with strings of words pushed out in a mood best described as panic.

The office chair creaks as you lean back, skipping songs until you find that perfect one. Crack your neck from side to side and yawn. As a new rhythm begins to play, your fingers drum on the cheap MDF. The other hand opens a new document. Your eyes pause on the harsh white screen, the cursor blinking expectantly back at you.

A blank page in need of 2000 words. You almost fucked the last essay for this module, turning in some semi-coherent piece 6 hours after it was due.

But this should be easy, just a short one and not due in till 12 tomorrow. You tell yourself this is simple. Just under 24 hours to write the lot and submit. That's less than 100 words an hour. You might even be able to squeeze a pint in tonight if you're smart about it.

First you need a title:

Self-reflexive commentary

Jesus.

As if the work you trudge through wasn't enough, now they want you to write about how you wrote a thing you hardly remember writing. Is there an academic term for saying, I pulled an all-nighter and came to with these words on the page?

The music builds in your ears. The mid-afternoon sun breaks through a crack in the curtain and splits your tiny room in half.

In this essay I will...

Pretend to have it together.

Take a deep breath and stretch your arms out then above your head. Arch your back into the chair, both of them creaking and straining.

It's the equivalent to a run-up.

Maybe that's all you need. One step back and a running start at the page. You dive back to your keyboard as if you were trying to catch it off-guard. For a moment your fingers race across the letters.

In this essay I will...

Stare at the cursor for a while, chasing fantasies of being good at any of this.

You hit the same wall again, your fingers refusing to make a single word materialise. You stare at them, lifting them to your face like that will encourage them to be good for a change, like the empty page is all their fault.

Bury your head in your hands and drag them down your cheeks. Come on, this one is easy. All you need to do is lie and make yourself sound like something other than fear fuelled this essay.

You should be good at lying about that by now.

Highlight the title, make it bold, underlined, *italicized*. Click file. Save As.

Another shit essay.

The track changes, a more upbeat melody parading around your empty page. It grows louder in the headphones, levels bordering on discomfort. You breathe in and exhale. Your body deflates in the chair, hands still hanging onto the keyboard.

Fuck, maybe you just need a drink. Water and a coffee to straighten out the senses. That's the one.

The chair rolls and skips to a stop on a stray black sock. Just a short break, five minutes if that. Then you'll take the essay on.

Before you know it, you're in the kitchen, staring at the kettle as it rattles to a boil on the counter. Swing open every cupboard in search of a single clean mug.

There's a pile of them scattered on the counter and in the sink, a couple of them growing spots of mould in the dregs of old tea. On the windowsill, three sponges rot next to an empty bottle of Fairy.

Check the fridge to find the only milk congealing in the bottle. In the cupboard, your cheap instant has turned hard. Crack at the solid block with a teaspoon then give up.

It doesn't get to you, in fact it's a welcome distraction. Just nod along to the song, each glimmer from the electronic beat building a wall between you and whatever the day throws at you. Grab your jacket and head out the door.

The heat of the December sun catches you off guard. You break into a little sweat as you take the shortcut through the park, dodging your way through a kick about between the lads in the flat below you.

The ball bounces and rolls your way. One of them shouts across the pitch. It practically lands by your feet, a perfect set up off the right foot.

You take a step back and give it a boot. The ball curls with laser precision straight through the hands of the two-cans-deep keeper. Walk away like it was nothing, the music rising to a crescendo in your ears.

Absolute fucking fluke. You know it, they know it, but that's not gonna break this high. You're on top form and the rest of this day is going to go down easy. You'll blast this essay, get some dinner then maybe even a pint. Surely, if you repeat the plan to yourself, it'll come true.

The song changes as you beep through the corner shop door. The guy behind the till keeps one eye on you as you stalk down the aisles.

Funky drums set the pace of your shop, a bassline adding a groove to each step. Milk first, then coffee. Fairy and sponges. Four Red Stripe. A pepperoni pizza and you're sorted.

You pay up and leave, taking the slightly longer route on the path around the park.

Push through the heavy fire door and head straight to the kitchen. No one else is in, or they're still in bed, so you've got the whole place to yourself.

Roll the sleeves on your jacket up and run the tap hot. Just a couple of mugs, that's all you'll do. Then right back to it. You set to work with the stiff sponge in hand.

The mugs and cups washed, you run a couple plates under the water and pile them to the side. May as well tackle the rest of them, while you're on a roll.

Scratching the sponge over a few chopping boards, all that's left is to leave the pans to soak. They need it too- you can hardly tell what's been cremated on the bottom of some of these.

Put the sponge over the counter, wiping the crumbs and flecks of weeks old food onto the floor. They crunch under the weight of your Docs as you trudge about the kitchen.

Great, you needed to write an essay and so far, you've done the shopping, played some footie and cleaned the kitchen.

Is there anything else you can do to not work? May as well grab a mop and bucket and go all in while you're at it.

Boil the kettle and grab the coffee from the plastic bag- the proper expensive Nescafé with the gold top. And why not, you deserve it after all the work.

Take a spoon to the foil. It snaps under the pulsing rhythm of music in your ears. Pour the water and let the aroma fill the space of the almost clean kitchen. Sure, you could've gone for some biscuits, but this'll do for now.

Back to it. You groove to your desk, nuzzling into the chair like you were settling in to watch a film or something. Gently place the mug in a perfect rectangle of dust from where the books for the last essay sat half-read for a month.

You pretend to take in the loose assembly of sentences on the page, but really you're half distracted by the song in your ears. For a second, there is bliss to be found. And it makes sense.

You've probably spent longer curating this playlist than you have on every essay combined. Each song is a perfect mood to zone out to and carry you through these long unwilling hours. There are no words, no lyrics, no voices; there are no distractions.

You glance at the word count to try justify an early dinner, but it's still dangerously under the 100-word mark. But it's not even 6 yet. That's what, 18 hours?

Easy enough if you stop pissing about.

Shrug off the thought and lean into the page.

In this essay I will...

Stall but get round to it eventually.

Don't look at the screen. Instead, keep your eyes fixed on your hands as they slowly punch the keyboard. The cursor jogs along the page.

Follow one lazy thought to the next. The rattle of the keys trails a string of half-truths and blatant lies behind it. It would be obvious to anyone who really knew you, but they can't expect good answers if they set stupid questions, can they?

The next time your eyes drift back to the screen, two paragraphs hang on the page. Sure, they're small and don't quite reach halfway, but it's a start.

You manage a large gulp of coffee which flares a sickly acid taste back up your throat.

You should probably eat something and soon.

Reflecting on my process, I would say...

Last minute panic is the world's greatest motivator and lowest achiever.

The oven whirrs to life, its orange glow breaking through the dark and blackened glass door. Through the sad hum of an acoustic guitar, you hear a low shuffle and a mumbled greeting. You drop an earphone out and look over your shoulder.

"Alright."
"Hey. You all good?"
"Yeah, I'm alright"
"Hungover to fuck though."

He grabs a glass from the drying rack and fills it with water. He turns on a slippered heel and shuffles back to his room. For a moment, you taste the lingering scent of vodka that's followed him home from last night.

It's not so different from an old folks home here on a Sunday. Everyone has gone too hard or hasn't stopped since Friday, and the fallout is like living with the old and dying, every single one of them just waiting for their time to end.

Is this what they imagined when they moved away from Mum and Dad? Is Uni just for the creeping realisation that most of adulthood is killing time and pretending to have a clue?

Reflecting on my process, I would say...

Time is only real when you're putting something off.

You open the fridge and stare at the four pack. Maybe just one with dinner would be alright. Think of it as a little Dutch courage to take on the rest of the essay. You're getting good at coming up with these excuses now. One beer loosens you up and helps get the creative juices flowing. A few cans helps you relax, and that means you'll work better tomorrow. You can't wind down properly without them. The internal arguments get easier to win every time, especially when everybody else is constantly wearing their hangovers as a badge of honour. Squeeze the fridge door and bite your lip.

Your hands ignore the back and forth in your head and tear one from the plastic ring. The crack of the can rings out through your one free ear, the other filled with the howling of a melancholy acoustic guitar.

A quarter of the beer goes down too easy. You pry open the oven and peer at the cheese on the pizza, just starting to bubble under the fan. The smell of a single charred chip wafts from the bottom of the oven. Sling the door shut and lean on the counter.

Drift into your phone, letting your thumb move aimlessly across the screen. Glazed eyes slide between pictures of your pals in the local back home, some lass from the year below standing on a beach doing a daft yoga pose and a picture of your dad in the garden.

Alone in the kitchen, a single thought washes over you, dumping your body on the shores of misery - looks like fun.

Your phone buzzes with a text.

Fancy a pint?

You should have seen this coming. There's always a pint going, especially when you're drowning in work.

Hell, they probably have stuff due also, so you should join in for a good moan about it. Tell yourself it would be good to get that feeling off your chest, instead of letting it fester in the room with you. It's not like you're doing any work here anyway.

Slide your phone in your pocket and check the pizza. You decide to get dinner in you first, and maybe try to get a few more words down. It's still early after all.

Slam about in the drawers for a pizza cutter and turn up with nothing. Finish your beer in a swig and look about the kitchen for a solution. A pair of black scissors lie discarded next to the hob.

Reflecting on my process, I would say...

There's more than one way to carve a pizza.

You crack another can open and pretend to read what you have on the page. It's like you don't recognise the words anymore, like someone else snuck in here and sketched up the beginnings of a shit essay. The important question now is how much you even care.

The way the module's weighted, it'd be hard to even scrape yourself above a 2:2. You'd be happy with that though, right? The way things are shaping up, it's probably your best shot. But none of that's even on the cards if you don't get the words down.

Lift a slice of pizza and burn the roof of your mouth in a single eager bite. You huff through the steam, refusing to give in. The skin blisters instantly. Settle it down with a swig of beer.

Your phone buzzes again, from the corner of your eye you catch his message.

??

Slide the phone in your hand and type out a response. Delete it and start again. Then once more. Finally, you nail it.

Where you thinking?

A perfect response. Open ended enough to back down, but just the right side of keen to say yeah, I fancy one. The reply comes.

Spoons in an hour?
Sounds good

It's not far from here, fifteen minutes if that. Could do a couple pints then straight back to finish this all off. That's what you tell yourself and you almost believe it.

Just bash out a couple hundred more words then off to the pub.

Your hands approach the keys like a drunk sauntering up to a karaoke; over-confident in the shit performance that is about to follow.

But to the credit of the beer and a half in your system, the words jump at the page. Sentences run on, clause after clause riding high on each other's backs. The number at the bottom ticks over.

Don't stop to think about it. There's no need to read any of it back. Just move forward. Another hundred words tick over, you feel almost competent.

If I could do anything differently...

There'd be more beer in the fridge.

Maybe this is a sweet spot, kind of like a game of pool in the local. All you need is just enough beer to be loose, but not enough to be sloppy. Another great excuse to avoid admitting the sheer relief you feel when a mouthful of beer instantly dampens the panic and the horrible thoughts that force their way into your head.

Cram a slice of pizza down, the rough edges scraping the numb skin on the roof of your mouth. Wash it down with beer. Toss the crust back on the plate. Empty the last of the can and chuck it in the bin by the bed. Do another slice. The prospect of another fresh can niggles at you. Its' a constant drip in the back of your mind.

Chew with your eyes half open, your fingers smashing out another paragraph of loosely constructed ideas. Surprise yourself when you check the word count.

998 words.

Nearly halfway and well deserving of that beer.

You glance over the haze of words, each paragraph descending into a mess of red squiggles. Lean back in your chair with your fingers locked behind your head. A deep burp ripples through your chest and hangs in the air. Your eyes linger for a moment more on that number in the corner.

998.

It sits there, taunting you.

Yeah, you're ALMOST halfway.

It shouldn't piss you off, but it does. You swing off the chair and pace the three steps you can fit inside the room. As the music plays, the walls seem like they're a little closer together.

You need fresh air, air and a couple of pints and you should be right as anything. Even if you don't write another word tonight, the panic of tomorrow should help you squeeze out another 1000 words.

But still those three digits sit there, unblinking.

May as well round it out, give yourself a cool thousand to settle on before heading out. Two words, that's all you need. Two lousy words you can delete in the morning before scrambling out the rest of it.

You've already fucked this module, and it's unlikely this shit essay will be enough to save you. The inevitable disappointment inches closer every second.

Lean over the desk and hammer the keys.

The door slams as you go for another beer. The cursor blinks beside two lone words hanging at the end of the page.

Academic Abattoir

LONELY BOY

Lonely boy living the life.

Another night at the bar, beer on tap, girl on his shoulder casually chatting the usual crap: dreams, friends, childhood, on and on why should I care.

Life stories isn't what I want us to share. Nod and smile, follow with a shot, just want to know if she is coming back to mine or not.

Why is it she persists in her noise.

I try to distance my mind but there is no other thought I can find than the idea that if the bar was empty and she were left here, would her stories continue to the mice and my half empty beer.

She makes my heart sink.

I think people like her will have it all in life when they become some millionaire's trophy wife, paraded around in style all the while the girls not so well wrapped must fight, so as not to be crapped upon by people like this moron.

The words glare back at you from the phone screen. The white page surrounds them and demands more from you. But right now, you have nothing, just these five words to sum up the churning in your gut.

Lonely boy, living the life.

You should take a marker pen and scrawl it in large capitals across the cubicle door. You should advertise them to the world, like every other hack writer in a shitty bar toilet.

07825565347 FOR GOOD TIME.
RYAN ~~HAS A BIG DICK~~ SUCKS COCKS.
I AM A LONELY BOY.

Instead, you save the draft, tuck your phone in your pocket and flush the handle with your foot. Two lads shuffle into the cubicle after you, mumbling in loud voices to each other.

"Give us that key pal."

You need to get back to the table and soon. You've not been in here long, and you doubt the other two have been keeping tabs, but you're treading the fine line between -

"There was a queue"
and
"I needed a shit"

Any longer and that's the impression you'll leave, a giant skid mark on the night. Run your hands under the tap for a second and let them drip under the wheeze of a hand dryer.

Stare at the reflection in the tiny, scratched mirror. There's a giant spot, right in the middle of your forehead. You gave it a good go before leaving and now you regret it. The icy wind and cold has erupted it into a giant ruby red stain on your pale white skin.

Someone in the cubicle takes a deep sniff, coughs and rustles the baggie to his mate. They talk in thick tones about some lass behind the bar.

"Fire in lad."
"You reckon?"
"Nowt to lose."

You push out the door wondering what type of wreck-head smashes gear on a Thursday.

Back in the bar and the place is getting busy, but it's mostly student types mixed in with the odd bewildered local.

Old men with poppies pierced on their coats scatter between the young screaming tables, their eyes fixed solely on the screen. They tut at every missed goal and sigh at every botched pass. A pint of bitter followed slowly by another.

The place is trying hard for that Budweiser themed sports bar, but they missed the mark by a country-fucking-mile. What they've ended up with is a shit Spoons with tacky neon and more green fields on screens than you could ever want.

You spot a gap at the bar and try to remember if there's enough of a pint waiting for you at the table. It's not your round though, at least you don't think.

No that's right, you got the first and the lass your mate knows, Dot, got the second. Just leaves him to get one now and you're all settled.

From across the way, you hear Dot's high pitched squeal mix with his chesty chuckle. God, even her laugh screams I'm from London.

You feel like shit but return to the table with a smile. Not a good smile, like I'm having a great time smile - more of a what did I miss type thing.

"Did you meet my pal that came up?"

Shake your head over a swig of ale. Nurse the sip down and swirl the head off the side of the glass.

"He's a fucking legend mate, honestly."
"Was he that weirdo who got kicked out of here?"
"Yeah, he's sound though."

An old man glances at you from a few tables over. You're all at least two beers louder than you were before you walked in. He shakes his head and turns to watch the screen again.

Those two pass a knowing glance across the drinks. There's a lot in the way they smile at each other, like the whole story of that night being told with a look.

Should you ask? No doubt they're gonna tell you anyway.

"Honestly mate…"

Here it comes…

"He's a sound lad."

She takes a swig of her pint and smiles as cool as anything.

"Aw, it's dead nice you've found someone."

She catches you off guard with that one. The two of you laugh. He furrows his eyebrows and shakes his head.

"Piss off."
"Honestly, you should see the way he looks at him."

She cups her hands next to her cheek and makes a kissy face. The laughs patter out and you each swig at the last of your drinks. You try think of something good to chime in with, but you've got nothing save for a knot in your throat.

Your stomach starts to throb a little. You can't tell if you just need another pint or some actual food. Turn to look at the bar and back to the table.

The phone buzzes in her hand and she dives into a message. He sees off the rest of his pint and slaps his knee.

"Right. I best be off."

You both stare at him as he starts to untangle headphones from his pocket.

"Ah come on. Stay for one more."
"Love to but I've got another 2000 words before tomorrow."

It's a hard one to argue with. The two of you are almost done for now, with just a couple exams you can pretend don't exist until after New Year.

He flings his Superdry on and does about a hundred different zips. She looks at her phone and thumbs another quick message. He flashes you a wink and nods his head to her.

"Text me when you get home safe."
"Will do Dot. Have fun you two."

He slings a rucksack over his shoulder and waves goodbye. As he pushes through the door and out into the dark snowy night, a piercing cold wind hits skin. Your eyes fix on the space he leaves behind. For the first time all night, you're not sure where to look.

She lays her phone on the table and puts her hair up in a ponytail. The hundred sports racing on every screen makes the bar look fast, but in reality everything is deathly still.

She sighs and settles her eyes on you.

"Does he always leave on his round?"
"Short arms and deep pockets with that one"

She chuckles and glances at another message on her phone.

You think back to the sly nod from your pal, just before he left. Maybe he's right. She's not gone yet, so the chance she is interested is probably good. Either way, you should get this round.

"I'll get us this one"

"Thanks. Think I'll go a G&T next. And could you see if they have cucumber instead of lime?"

You repeat the order back to her and sling your body up and over for the next round.

There's only a handful of people standing at the long bar, but the two of them on the other side are struggling. Glasses clatter and beer spills over the rim as they scramble around each other. They're about the same age, but he swaggers his gut behind the bar like a true manager type.

The red hair lass's hand slips as she lifts an empty off the side. It cracks off the wood and smashes on the ground. The whole place erupts in a collective -

"WAHEY!"

48

He's on the clean-up before she even has a chance to process what's gone on. She shakes her head and turns to you, her cheeks burning with each sweep of broken glass.

You blurt out your order as some old guy at the other end starts to shout about how he was next on. She gives him the side eye; he mumbles to himself and backs down.

"Single or double?"
"Single, thanks"

You tune out to the rugby on the screen as a player lines up for a conversion. Hard to place the teams, probably some Italian league that only exists inside these types of bars.

He scuffs his run to the ball and sends it flying just-right of the post. The camera zooms in on his pissed expression as he runs back to his half. Before you know it, two drinks are thrust under your nose.

You pass a twenty across and put the change back in your wallet. It's getting heavier in coins with every round, the thin stack of notes reduced to a single twenty now. That was your cash for the week, and you've pissed it away, again.

Weave between the regular boozers, the pockets of students and the odd lonely man. Meanwhile she sits in the far corner of the place, head buried in the phone.

The guys from the toilet stall are a few tables down, giving her the eye and scanning the place for who she could be with. Lay the drinks in front of her and take a seat. Give the guys a casual look and they turn their backs to you.

She looks up from the screen at the slice of lime nestled between thick cubes of ice.

"No Cucumber then?"

"Nah, sorry"

One simple order and you fucked it. But then again, who asks for cucumber in a drink. This isn't London.

She takes the short straw and fishes the lime out, flicking it onto a napkin on the table. She swirls the ice around and talks to the glass.

"Can't do lime anymore"
"Yeah?"
"Too many tequila slammers at socials."
"Yeah, they're grim"

You both pause to get that first sip down you. The sighs of relief are synchronised, a little extra fuel to make the conversation go down easy, or so you'd think.

She pauses on another long sip of gin. Maybe you should ask her about...

"Honestly, those hockey socials are brutal. Like I must have spent half my loan on snakebite."
"You drink that stuff?"

"I don't choose to, just what you do though."

Not you. Sure, you signed up for a couple societies, but the chances were always slim you'd turn up for anything other than the odd party. What was it you said about them that time?

"I don't need a Drama Soc to drink"

"They're a good bunch though, those girls."

50

"I bet"

"You play anything?"

You used to. Every weekend for years, your dad would wake the house up early on a Sunday and drive you and your brothers to the rugby club. You'd always be the first ones there, the four of you sat in the clubhouse with a round of bacon butties.

Once those tiny shoes slotted on your feet, your dad would tie them on for you. To this day, you probably still couldn't do them the way he did, laces strung tight and looped around the shoe. After he did that double knot, it felt like there was nothing on your feet at all.

But that was when you didn't have to think any further than the end of the day or whether you had any homework for tomorrow.

But once high school started and the other teams got bigger, the pitch eventually gave way to other things- girls, friends, parties and how much booze you could nick from under your dad's nose.

"Nah not really"

"You should come down for hockey practice sometime."

"You reckon?"

"Honestly, they're always looking for people."

"Maybe, yeah"

She's like a walking advert for the Uni Experience. You can almost picture her on the front of some leaflet now; hockey stick in hand, a kit stained in sweat and her top lip bulging with the gum guard.

She's either holding a trophy in her other hand or has her arms looped around a couple of teammates. The banner behind them says something like -

Win friends with Hockey Soc.

And once again you've let the silence go on for too long. You need to get it together, there's no chance of any of this if you keep it all in your head. You need to make conversation.

Your stomach twists again, leaving you to hide your grimace behind another swig of ale. Ask her something stupid like -

"Where are you from again?"

You both look dumfounded by the question. She smiles and answers anyway.

"I'm actually from Putney, in London."

You nod along as if you know anything about the place at all.

"Sounds Nice"
"It is, yeah."

She nods a little matter-of-factly about it. You pull down another hit of ale then lean in a little. For a second, you let yourself feel good about something.

"I'm not being funny but South London is the best place for a night out."

A chair scrapes from the table behind her. A real old timer shakes his walking stick across the floor and strains himself into the seat.

"There's just like, always something going on."

He slides a ratty handkerchief out and blows his nose. You try focus in on what she is saying but it's difficult. There's something almost hypnotic about the way he moves in the corner of your eye. Like when he blinks, it almost surprises him where he is.

"But you know, right, moving here wasn't as bad as I thought."

The old man lays his hand on the table and checks his watch. He turns his head to look around the bar, but it's anyone's guess how much he can see through his heavy-set eyes. A smile lights up every wrinkle on his face.

"Cos you know back in London, I had like the best set of friends."

An old dear shuffles across the floor, probably the same age as him but with a good bit of life in her step still. She's got a Guinness in one hand, wine in the other.
The man grounds his walking stick and steadies himself to his feet. He does a short run around the table and untucks her chair.
She smiles and lays the drinks on the table. He looks exhausted by the time he drops to his seat again.

"Like I would do anything for those girls. We still talk, like every day."

You've both seen off a good bit of your drinks by now. She smiles and rests her arm on the table, toying with a beermat. Maybe it's a sign, maybe it's absolutely nothing.

"And I know they would do anything for me."

You think about the faces you knew back home. It's a trick of all the social media really, to think that you're keeping up when really all you're doing is staring at one another. When last did you even send one of them a message?

"Yeah, I get that."

She inches her glass across the table, smearing a ring of water across the wood. She leans over her drink and sucks the last of the gin from between the ice, the slurp cutting through the hum of the bar.
She smiles and stabs the straw into the ice-cubes.

"One more?"
"I've got this one."

What the hell are you doing? You know you don't have the money to turn down a free pint.

"You sure?"
"Yeah, it's no problem. Same again?"

She looks a little surprised by this.

In fairness, you can't remember the last time someone bought a pint for you without the expectation of one in return. Everyone is poor as shit, the next loan payment just a little too far away to share anything other than a laugh.

"No lime."
"No problem"

She smiles and instinctively reaches for her phone as you walk away.

There's this small moment, just before reaching the bar, when you feel a warm buzz through your body. In the months since you arrived, you've forgotten what it feels like to be free of the dead weight. But the flicker of feeling passes almost as quickly as it arrives. It's like your head floats as you cut between tables, every step twisting the warm sensation to a dull weight in your chest.

You lean against the bar as the heavy manager lines up a dozen Jaeger bombs for some lads in training gear beside you. They slip their fingers in the rim and carry them back to a group on one of the bigger tables.

Through the hum of drinkers and the flashes of a dozen screens, you pull your own phone out and open the page again.

There isn't a thought in your mind that you could fill on this page. There is only you, the bar and the girl from London who wants cucumbers in her gin.

Look back through the hive of booze to your table. She's talking on the phone, her hands waving as if someone was sat right across from her. It's hard to tell if she smiles when she turns and catches your eye.

The manager slumps himself over.

55

"What you on pal?"

You shout the order and turn to look at the screen again. The page is still empty, but your fingers refuse to move, as if there was something stopping them. They hover over the barren page. You know the words but it's like they disappear in the space between your head and the phone.

He lays the drinks across from you, a tall gin sparkling on the bar with a thick wedge of lime buried in the ice. Slide your phone away and pass him the last note in your wallet.

You stare at the two drinks, the small bubbles leaping out of the tall glass of gin and landing on the bar. You should ride this out, see where it goes.

Maybe there'll be nothing. Maybe something. Either way, it's better than drinking alone.

WHO I MIGHT BE

Hidden from the streets of sleet, up a close and in a flat 'semi-furnished', the party caldron is on the boil. Rising voices and wall wobbling music draw in the young who will live forever and repel those who feel forever is just too long. I batter down the door, eager to be immortal for the night.

In the swirling spitfire dog fight of cultures, cliques and clichés I revel, free to escape the confines of who I am and allow my imagination to dictate who the people around me shall meet tonight. The frantic magic that is friendship for only a few hours.

Enter the first room to see the stoners and the loners
speaking their Merry-Jane manifesto to all those that
will listen, the bong-based theories of repression and
conspiracy. They shall meet the revolutionary, young,
volatile an anti-state anarchist. A man of speeches and
schemes, to lead them and their pipe, to a deserved
salvation.

Queens of the kitchen will meet the marvellous mystery
man in dire need of the analysis and care only these
Glenn's girls can provide. They will see a boy with
defences unbreakable by all but them. A fictional drama,
to play the part of the honey in the beehive.

Finally, we have the clan driven Vikings drinking from
antiques and enjoying the inhibition free fun of the kings
cards made tarot for the night. I sit with my bottle as the
national drinking champion and join the laughter and
language.

Drunk and alone I stagger home, lost in a city I know
well. My journey takes hours or minutes impossible to
tell but now I find myself once again in my bed and as I
fade, I wonder who I might be tomorrow.

Four beers deep, your body doesn't shrink against the cold but embraces it. A sharp wind snaps against your cheek. Chest puffed out, a deep breath runs through your body. The exhale drifts and fades into the dark sky.

The street lingers through the night, each step a burst of mud-shit sleet beneath your boots. Cradle the bottle of vodka in the crook of your arm like a sleeping child. You can't feel your fingers, but it's not far now.

A siren beckons from the weekend streets far behind you. It rips through the cold silence. Your eyes shut for a moment as the wailing ekes further into the distance.

Picture the blue flashes echo through the busy streets, the flushed red faces and coarse voices clambering from one pub to the next.

You leave it behind like footprints in the snow.

A streetlight casts a long shadow on dormant cars. You tightrope along white lines in the middle of the road, the sleeping flats around you looking on through curtain-shut eyes.

The great performer. Entertainer. A spotlight surrounds you.

Applause and blaring horns.

"Out the road you fucking wanker."

A taxi screeches past. The driver gives the finger and the women in the back screech with laughter. But it doesn't get to you.

Somewhere up ahead, muffled bursts of bass ripple through the empty streets. Take a right and work your way past tight packed cars into a small close.

From the tower of flats above you, blurred voices escape an open window and echo off the empty street. Flashes of red and green throw shadows of bodies against the wall inside.

Something like embarrassment washes over you. You drag your feet as slowly as possible as you reach the door propped open with a brick.

It's not too late to turn around, but you shake off the idea and step inside. You know better than anyone that you need this.

Take the stairs two at a time. Hammer a frozen hand on the door, wait a second, then go inside.

You are swallowed by the music into the night.

***

Brush off the outside world and drop your coat in a pile somewhere. Heads in the hall turn. No one they know- they turn back. You head through the kitchen door and find the only face you recognise.

He smiles and gives you a half-drunk squeeze of a hug.

"Sorted for drinks pal?"

Smile and shake the bottle of vodka. Laughter and shouts erupt from the hall outside. He finds you a clean glass from a cupboard, clearly stolen from a pub somewhere.

Eyeball the vodka then use the dregs of a coke bottle. No ice. Flat. Almost warm. Still perfect.

He takes you through to the crowded hallway. The slight swell from the alcohol blends with the music and the cacophony of voices. You feel a rise of hot blood in your cheeks.

He stops in the hall and turns to point behind you.

"Kitchen. Toilet. Smoke in there."

A girl you half recognize from Uni bursts out of a door and throws her arms around him. He picks her up and spins her round, while you drift further and further into the background.

A new song starts blaring behind one of the doors, they cheer and run inside. Suddenly you are alone, nursing slow sips of shit vodka.

The kitchen is a mob of inward conversations. You scan the room to see where you might fit in. A couple of recognisable faces but not a single name you know. You keep searching for an in somewhere but find nothing.

As you slide back through the hallway, a sweaty arm lands
on your shoulder. Before you have time to turn around, he
slurs your name into your ear.

"Alright"

You pull back and take him in. Thursday morning lectures.
He's the guy that always comes late and sits on his phone at
the back. At least, he was there for the first few weeks. He
looks like he's almost completely given up.

His hair is damp with sweat and he stinks of stale fags.
There's a beer in each hand and half of one down his shirt.

Two girls standing nearby smirk as they go past but he doesn't
even notice.

He yells about how much of a great time he's having. You
nod in agreement but you both see through it. He juggles the
beers in one hand and reaches into his pocket for a crumpled
deck of fags.

He thrusts them towards you. Hell, why not? Slide one out
the pack and behind your ear. Follow him through the door at
the end of the hall.

Heavy air bubbles under bongs, smoked up and blown
vaguely toward the window. LED lights charge the room in a
slow oscillation of reds, blues and greens. Squint eyes and
heavy breaths greet you.

Numb hands return to feeling with sharp needles
underneath the skin. You feel it in your cheeks too, like the
face you turned up with is slowly pricked and moulded by the
temperature.

Someone budges to the side on a cushion. You step over
cross legged bodies and ashtray cans, find a spot against the
wall and crouch on the carpet. Blink and there's a joint in your
hand.

You take a hard pull, your face ignited in a harsh orange glow. Hold it for 3... 2... Exhale. Pass it on.

On the sofa across from you, half slouched bodies work in factory lines, turning out lit joints and passing them on. Small exchanges of strains and weight pepper the air around them.

A face you half recognise from the back of a lecture hall stumbles up from the bed on the far end and out the room.

The smoke seems to swirl behind her, before a harsh yellow light and bass overflow from outside and cut through the low energy in the room. The guy next to you chokes on the inhale and hacks his lungs into his hand.

You're only one drag into the night, but you feel it push its way through every muscle of your body. Limbs and eyes feel a little heavy now. The minute it hits the cheap vodka buzz, your whole being goes into a numb smile. The sense of relief is so overwhelming it's almost scary.

The guy next to you stops coughing long enough to crack open a can of Dragon Soup. You taste the sweet stench between breaths of dense air.

Your eyes tune out and ears tune in to a conversation on the other side of the room.

"That's what I'm saying though, no one ever talks about the real power struggle."

You get up and find a place on the bed near them. Five bodies camp around an ashtray on the duvet, nursing drinks and passing joints between them.

"Like if you follow the money..."
"...you see who's really in charge."
"Fuck, they're all corrupt anyway."
"True, True."

"The problem is us too though."

61

You're just as surprised by your voice as they are. The circle moves their eyes to you, sussing you out through their vacant stares. As you start to speak, you try for a more earnest expression through the stoned glaze of your eyes.

"The longer we play by their rules, the more we validate them."

The lass next to you passes a joint on. You make a point of flourishing the lit end as you talk. It's all nonsense, but they hang off every word.

"Exactly. That's why they keep winning. We keep playing a game they make the rules for."

Nod along over another toke and pass the joint on. Launch into another string of meaningless sentiments.

"But at the end of the day, it doesn't matter who wins or loses. Nobody wants any real change. They want to keep on playing."

The faux intellectual thing is playing well with this crowd, but is it really you?

"What can you do though?"

Yeah, what can you do?

"We can play a different game."

****

Back in the kitchen, the air feels lighter and the people more vivid. Lean on the counter and clutch the drink tight.

It's a better vibe in here. The front door slams and three girls from your block walk in, coats on and drinks unopened in carrier bags.

"Hiya mate!"
"How're you doing?"

Not drunk enough to make an arse of it, not too stoned that you act like a zombie.

"All good, yeah"

You step inside the group and perch on the table. They sit around you with a chorus of bursting cider cans.

"You stop somewhere before then?"
"Aye we just stopped at our pals for pre drinks.
        They're off to another gaff though.
                Might come later if it's shit."
"Probably see them later then."

They laugh at that. Swirl your drink and see it off, taking the moment to think of something else to say. One of them cuts in.

"I think I saw you the other night."

You lift your eyebrows and watch the reaction of the other two. They pass some look back and forth.

"It looked like you were having fun."

She smiles like she caught you out. You smile like it was nothing.

"Yeah, that may have been me."

Faintly, you still smell the perfume. The taste of her cocktail tongue moving through your mouth. The cold wind on the walk home. A sad Hawaiian pizza.

"Didn't see you leave..."
"...Must have slipped out early..."

Out in the hallway, your pissed up mate stands slack against the wall, waiting for the toilet to free up. He finishes up the drink in his hand and stares open mouthed at the locked door.
You drift back into the group. They've moved on, laughing about someone's diabolical dancing on the night in question.

"Like picture you're uncle at a wedding...
    ...but he's gurning out his nut."

Laugh with them, shaking your head like you're in on the joke.

"Honest to god..."
"I've never seen a person sweat so much."
"Oh, I saw Dot earlier...
    ...She was asking after you.
        ...Wanted to know if you'd be here.
            You should send her a text."

The other two pause to give a secret smile, finally settling their eyes on you. The full weight of the room bears down, squeezing anything like nerves out the soles of your feet.
Stall and twirl the empty glass on the table. Smile like this happens a lot.

"Oh right"

Your ears throb, like they want to exit this conversation early.

"Yeah, I'll drop her a line."
"Are you and her...?"

You shake your head and dangle the bait of her name above their heads.

"I like Dot but I dunno whether it's just...you know?"
"Well, I reckon..."

And with that, their wisdom on how to conquer love stretches into the night.

****

Slump into the wall and focus on a point on the floor to stop the spinning. Your unwanted friend slides over. He grins at you with black teeth like some low-budget vampire and pushes a bottle of red wine into your hands.

You consider for a second, pretending to read the label. Too much of anything is barely enough. Your stomach flips as the four quid red hits it with a burst of acid. But it takes the edge off a little.

You're almost coasting now. Just need a quick break. The toilet door opens and you dive in before anybody cuts in front of you.

Lock the door and breathe. A splash of cold water on your face gives you a bit of life. Scoop up a few handfuls and slurp them down. As you stare into the mirror, you almost convince yourself the person looking back is having a good time.

Two furry specks of black mould in the top corner of the room catch your eye. They're only small. They can be wiped off, but they won't be. They'll be left to grow until they form a thick mass, spores leaking out and sitting in the lungs, spreading their tendrils through your body and suffocating you.

After the year is over, the landlord will paint over it. For a brief while it'll be gone, but the moisture in the paint will only feed it and it will grow through stronger. Year on year it'll build until it engulfs the whole place.

Someone's banging on the door like they can't just -gimme a minute-

Did you bring your drink in here? The hell were you even on now? You burp and taste beer. Must be on the cans. You lift a couple of suspect tins resting on the sink and windowsill and leave with the fullest one.

The door gets bum rushed by two girls the minute you unlock it. It slams behind you. Water rushes as you push on down the hall of bleary faces, finding the door where the music plays loudest and push inside.

****

The tallest of the lads lays the thing on the table and cracks half a can in. What the fuck would you even call it? Somewhere between a tankard and a vase. It sits in the middle of the table surrounded with a mess of cards.

"Ring of fire everyone."

Nothing good ever comes of this game, but you find yourself in the circle, unable to leave the huddle of guys filling the room. One by one they take a card, the forfeits shouted by the tall guy.

Wait your turn then pull a card and hold it to the group. All their hands shoot into the air, leaving you the odd one out. The tall lad points at your can.

"Down the rest of it mate."

Finish your drink. Grab another can from the floor and crack it open. Cider rots your teeth and gags you with a sickly-sweet sting.
Someone leans over and stares into the drink in the middle.

"Who put wine in?"
"Left hands yah cheating bastard."
"Elbows touch the floor. What was that new rule?"
"I don't know, what was the rule?"
"Do you know?"
"Aye, it's..."

Why the fuck are they cheering? Some haircut in charity shop clothes sees his drink off. Your turn again, take a card.

"3. 2. Waterfall..."

For a hard minute, the room goes quiet.
Stale-fag-shit-beer-stain calls you by your name. Someone pops open a stubby and tips his head back.

"In one pal."
"Four cards left yah fuckers."
"Then some cunts on that shit hot mess."

You ever seen a drink so shit it froths?
Only four cards left now and it's your go.

67

Pull the last King. A cheer erupts. Everybody's glad it's not them. You move towards the jug, trying to look as if you're dreading it. In reality, you're relieved it's you. Your head is filled with thousands of voices, all screaming at you to give up. It's getting harder and harder to drown them but you think this might just do it, for tonight at least.

They're cheering now. Hands slap together. The tall guy leans over a table and starts banging a drum roll.

You lift it high above your head like a crowning glory of the night. Steady yourself with three deep breaths. They clap and stomp out your name. Someone slides in through the door.

Open your throat and tip your head back. Don't let it touch your tongue. Don't think about stopping. Can't take a break. Needs to be in one. Just focus on finishing. Ignore the fizz crawling from your stomach.

The ripple of hands settle as the room collectively gags on your behalf. Someone in the room whispers your name in conversation.

The dregs slide down your throat. Hold it upside down above your head, the last drops falling on your scalp and dripping down your face. Stick your tongue out like a child with his medicine.

You soak in the victory, random lads slapping your back and hugging you close in their damp heavy arms. Smile and let yourself turn around with arms cast wide.

A sharp burp rushes the taste back. Your mouth fills with saliva, ready to throw it all back out. Hold it down with a —

"Fucking have some of that!"

Something churns and croaks in your throat.

Dot stands in the doorway, grimacing at the man in the middle of the room. She turns her back on you and leaves. The game ends and the night goes on.

****

There's a strange crossover of endings and beginnings. As you pass the bus stop, you see weary eyed workers waiting for another day of drudgery, trying not to make eye contact with the washed-up leftovers of the night before.

Your shoulder rams into something hard. Shop shutters clatter through the peaceful silence and the headache starts to set in.

Further down the road, you spot a familiar face, sitting against a bin, still clutching the bottle of red wine. His head flops back and forth and he mumbles something as you approach him. Shake him by the shoulder and he wakes up, startled by his surroundings.

He manages to get up with a little help. Ask him where he lives and he gestures in the opposite direction. You watch him for a few moments as he sways off into the distance.

The buzz is fading and you can feel the general ache spreading through your body- a warning of the grim day to come.

Eventually, you see the squat halls at the end of the long road. On the way back you try to get ahead of the hangover and stop into a corner shop for some Lucozade and paracetamol. Throw some down on the way home and chug the fizzy orange. It won't work, but at least you tried.

Your halls are quiet when you get back, the dim blue light of the morning just about leaking in through the windows.

Everybody's either out or not up yet. You sit in the kitchen for a few minutes, absorbing the quiet and sipping at a glass of water. The vibrant feelings of a few hours ago have disappeared and you're left with the dull equilibrium and a soft ringing in your ears.

Back inside your room you notice a small patch of mould, growing through from the ceiling. You lie there, staring at it, willing yourself to go to sleep.

ANGER

A fog on my mind and a vice on my heart, bullet fast blood with friction heat rushes to cramping muscles and a blinding wish to tear this last year apart.

Picking at the fraying seam and revel as it unravels, dump the tangled memory mess on a fire to forget and

70

*let the strands turn to carbon ash black with the back
lash of lingering hate.*

*Hate for the guise of a friend, a liar protected by gender
who slashed and ground at my trust from the start, a
heartless tart in the clothes of a saint and what's worse
is that I bought it hook line and sinker.*

*Just as I fancied myself the great interpreter, lover and
deep thinker I actually played the part of a witless prick.
Rose tinted specs shattered I can hear the shrill pitch of
her pied piper song leading me and the other guys
goaded into going along for the same ride.*

*All of us falling for the tears and perfect mask made to
reflect a dream that might come to pass as long as we
bow down and accept this self-respect fatality.*

*Now humiliated, a wounded beast, I let the witch escape
to leave me pining before realising I was left in the
stocks, only then becoming aware of the bruises, from
rocks, hurled at my pride. Every false smile, promise,
touch and show of affection fuels my aggression and
desire to be rid of this crutch of sickening intent that I
carry myself on until every second of caring I showed the
bitch is burnt and gone.*

Barrel into the room, letting the fire door slam behind you.
Pace up and down trying to shake the feeling that burns over
your skin. Your cheeks and ears are crimson red, a knot in
your throat so tight you think you might be sick.

You never should have left this shithole of a room in the
first place. You bared all to her, put your trust in her and she
reeled you along and left you dangling.

After she disappeared at that party you didn't give her another thought, but seeing her today, a chance encounter in the Union, left you empty. When a person is as lost as you are, the smallest hint of anything that looks like hope is enough to latch onto.

It's so easy to get lost inside your own head and project a narrative onto the world. That chance meeting and everything that followed must have been leading to something.

The flashed smiles when nobody was looking, the brushes on your arm. All lines in a story you were writing in your own mind. The final chapter was all mapped out.

It ended with her dragging you out of this hole and pointing you in the right direction. You would emerge from your cocoon of self-pity and finally find your way back to the person you were before.

You did everything right. But maybe all the obvious signs were ignored as you fixated on the small details that fit the narrative.

That's why you're angry. She's just another path that leads to more fruitless hope. She should have known better, that's what you tell yourself as you kick the bin in the corner and send empty cans rattling across the carpet. But even then, you know that this is a lie.

You're not angry with her. All the shame and emptiness that's been building for months was all projected on her. She was supposed to be your way out, but now she just represents another failure. You're not angry that she rejected you, you're angry that she gave context and words to all those abstract feelings.

That monster growing inside you can be ignored sometimes. Don't look it directly in the eye, shut out the creeping footsteps with a pair of headphones or a night of excess. Keep running and it won't catch you.

But she threw a mirror up in your face and made you look directly at it. All the stories that you created about being worthless and letting down everybody around you became true in an instant. Rejection made them tangible, a bolt of anxiety and shame ripping through you.

You had a choice then, you could have faced it head on, stared it down and admitted the reality that you needed help, that things were gradually drifting further from your grip, your old self fading to a mere speck on the horizon.

You fall onto the bed and stare into the ceiling. The emotions ebb and flow, interspersed with a numbness much deeper than you've ever felt before. All the dirt of life courses through your body. A thick sludge, sapping the feeling from the world. It needs to be purged.

You tried so many times to drown it out, but it always resurfaces. It always gets worse. If you could throw it all out there, maybe you'd feel better. Like the relief you feel after throwing up a beer you didn't need. Lay those feelings bare, not for somebody else, for nobody. Send them out into the world and be rid of them.

You reach into your pocket and pull out your phone. The harsh blue screen draws you in as you shut everything else out. Open the notes and flick through the library of half formed poems. All your most difficult emotions turned into the seeds of something beautiful. This is your refuge, your own form of therapy, hidden from the world as you silently hammer away at the keyboard.

You start a new note and the words hit the screen instantly. They pour out of you and twist themselves into musical sentences, one line jumping to the next. You don't think about what you're writing, it just comes out, as if it's flowing through you from somewhere else.

The dense mass inside your head begins to break apart. Your muscles loosen and the tightness in your chest washes away. The lines are a bit stunted, some of the transitions are sloppy, but it doesn't matter.

It's all falling out of you, all the horrible shit you carry has direction now. It's turning into something dark but beautiful, like a lion tearing apart a gazelle.

With each keystroke, the sense of excitement builds. The worst parts of yourself are no longer in control, trapped instead in metaphor and honesty. Seeing it laid out like that is liberating. It all shrinks down and becomes simple words that could easily be deleted if you wanted to.

Eventually, the momentum dies down. You throw the phone on the bed and breathe deeply. For a few moments, you feel quiet. Bask in the lightness that you rarely experience.

As you pick up the phone and read it back, the words feel like they're somebody else's. It's no longer your burden because you threw it on the page and cut yourself free. It exists in an empty space, never to be seen by anybody. A Pandora's box of ignored feelings and from time to time you peek inside it, poking at what's there.

Scrolling through the collection, you see a collage of the last months of your life. Through these words, you see a person you barely recognise anymore.

If you showed them to somebody, maybe they could see through it to the person hiding behind them. All the false smiles and reassurances would fall away, and they'd see that you needed help. But the thought of anybody else reading those words fills you with dread.

Even though it's the one thing keeping you going, you still see it as something to be ashamed of. It doesn't fit with people's idea of who you are. Would they really see it as an opportunity to help or would it just be another disappointment?

You're a man, you have to stick to the accepted methods for dealing with life.

Pull your socks up, have a pint. Laugh it off, deflect it, convince yourself it isn't real. Have another pint. Have six more. Throw a few shots in the mix and try your luck with somebody at a club. Wake up in the morning and blame your rotten feelings on the drink. Rinse and repeat.

It's still better than sharing it with somebody. So, you just keep pouring it out into that secret library in your phone, praying that one day, things will get better.

The relief never lasts long. In the moment, it helps you detach and try to make sense of the world. It's cathartic to purge yourself in those stolen moments at the back of a bus or hidden away in your room. But locking it away doesn't work, it just delays things. It won't be long until you find yourself back here.

Your tour through the failures of the past months is interrupted by a text.

Did you get a Christmas present for mum?

Shit. In amongst the essays, shame-filled hangovers and apathy, you forgot all about Christmas. Mustering the energy to do something thoughtful seems impossible right now. Push it aside, work something out later. You've still got a few days until you head home for the holidays.

You were supposed to be enjoying the freedom from endless essays and constant stress. But that's all out of the window now. Instead of ending the term on a high, you ended it with a predictable disappointment.

Just a few more days until you return home and face your friends and family. The hallways outside your room buzz with anticipation. People can't wait to get back and tell stories of their amazing experience. They'll return triumphant, welcomed by proud parents and friends that are jealous they decided not to apply.

But their old favourite pubs won't feel the same, not now that they've moved onto better things. The first few days will feel nostalgic and comfortable, but it won't be long until they're itching to get back to their own lives, the ones that they carved out themselves instead of growing into by chance.

Their parents will pack them off to the train station again, smiling as they tell themselves they've done a good job, happy in the knowledge their children have grown into adults and made it on their own. They wait eagerly to see what successes lies ahead.

But it won't be like that for you, at least that's not what you think. You're wrong, but you can't help but convince yourself your trip home will be like lining up in front of the firing squad.

So many sleepless nights have been spent wishing you could be back home, when things were simpler. But you know that world is gone forever now.

Home won't be comforting - it'll be a minefield of questions you don't want to answer. Nights will be spent catching up with old mates and listening to them rattle on about how amazing it all is. You'll nod along, hiding behind your pint and pretend that you're having the same experience.

Still, you'd better start packing. Push yourself from the bed and start swinging your arms over the carpet, scooping the beer cans and empty takeaway boxes into the bin. Drag a hand across the desk and scrape all the dusty crumbs onto the top of the pile.

A dog-eared essay hides under the pile of crap. You pull away a couple of crisp packets to reveal the sea of red scribbles. Reading over the comments you can't help thinking that your lecturer was generous with her marking.

Sure, it's still a fail, but she tried so hard to find something positive to say about the mess of half-formed bullshit you turned in. Stuff it in the back of your rucksack and chuck it on the floor.

Crack a window open, it's freezing but you need to get rid of that thick damp smell. You stand by the open window for a moment and look through the heavy sheets of rain.

Water hammers against the windowsill and sends a spray into your face. Enjoy it for a second, lean out a little and let the water wash over your head. Stare into the ground below and watch people hurry back and forth, hunched in with hoods pulled over their heads. Cool fingers of rain brush the back of your neck and you shiver.

Pull your head in and turn back to the half-packed room, strewn across the carpet. With as little urgency as possible, you start picking up items here and there and throwing them into bags and suitcases. A t-shirt, stained with pizza from the time you fell asleep eating in bed. Ripped jeans from a fall down the steps at the back of a club. Rifle through the pockets and pull out a handful of coppers and soggy receipts.

Unfold one and scan through the checklist of shit decisions and wasted money. Throw them in the general direction of the bin and carry on sorting through the mess.

****

A few hours later, you find yourself marching through the rain on the way back from the off license. It soaks you, fighting each step as you trudge back towards your room with a carrier bag of cans in your stinging red hand.

You've made a good start on packing, might as well relax for a bit. There's a couple of days left and no more work to be done, for now at least.

You hear the beginnings of a party when you get back to the halls. A couple of guys rummage around in the kitchen cupboards, pulling out unwanted lagers and the dregs of spirits leftover from long forgotten parties. It'll all get mixed up and thrown down in a last hurrah as they mourn the end of the first term. You won't join them. You just slip in with a quick nod and grab some leftover Chinese from the fridge before sloping back to your room.

That knot in your stomach never really goes away. It writhes around, fuelled by shit food and too much drink, lurching up into your throat whenever you feel a rush of anxiety come over you.

Right now, as you sit there, thinking about the prospect of facing your family again, it grips you tight. It's like there's a weight inside, pulling everything into a twisted mass and ripping away at whatever small part of you is left. Eventually, you're unrecognisable.

But at least you're hidden away. In some strange way, you're comfortable here. If you're locked behind that door with distance between you and everybody else, you're safe.

Only the scribbled notes in your phone get a real look in. But you can't stay hidden forever. You'll have to show yourself soon. And all that promise and aspiration that you left home with- will they notice how it's gone?

Take a deep breath in, hold it for a second, then exhale. Scrunch your fists up and think logically. They're your family, they'll always support you, they only want you to be happy.

You're right, but in that moment, you can't hold onto the idea. It dissipates as quickly as it was formed, and the knot tightens. Grab the can, neck it and open another.

****

The next couple of days are spent locked in your room, only venturing out for food and more drinks. The sound of parties drifting down the hallways gets quieter each night as more people filter out and head for home.

During the day, the silence is punctured by the occasional door slam or muffled conversation but mostly, you're alone. Hours disappear in front of your laptop, staring through TV shows you've watched a thousand times, rolling on episode after episode until you fall asleep in front of them.

You could have gone home earlier, when you finished all your essays, but you've still got a small stash of cash left that has stretched you this far.

You did the maths and managed to keep yourself in frozen pizza and cans for another few days and still have money left for train fare. But the well is all dried up, your tickets are booked, and tomorrow, you head for home.

A bulging rucksack and a hand-me-down suitcase sit in the corner with all your stuff crammed in. The laptop plays into the night.

Wake up and tune into the credits of the show, still rolling. Slam the lid and check the time. Not long to make it to the station, no time for a shower. Push the laptop into a gap in your rucksack, find a space in the suitcase for the charger. Add the empties to the pile in the bin and head out.

As you close the door to your room and lock it, you stop for a second. Imagine yourself opening it again to find an empty room, a blank canvas. A chance to do it all again. In some ways, you don't want to leave. You're in limbo in that room, moving nowhere. Being detached feels safe, even though you know it isn't.

The walk to the train station is bitter. Snow drifts onto the pavement and melts into the thick slush. Your boots slam on the ground, kicking it out to the sides. The suitcase wheels spray up the back of the jeans, but you ignore the stinging around your ankles and push on, hoping you don't miss your train. Not because you want to get on it, but because you can't afford to buy another ticket. Asking to borrow the money would only make things worse.

The station is chaotic when you arrive, filled with disgruntled travellers, annoyed that hordes of students have invaded their usual train. You float through the excitement of people heading home to visit family or travelling to their last day of work before two weeks off.

Put your head down and dodge through the crowd. The train is waiting at the platform. Everybody huddles around the door, primed and ready with their suitcases. They watch for an opening as people pile out, everybody hoping to find the gap first and get a spot for their luggage. You wait at the back of the pack and by the time you climb aboard, the racks are packed with cases like a game of Tetris.

All the seats are gone, and you resign to sitting on your case in the no-man's land between carriages. Put your headphones in. The train rattles on and you fall into a dead state, occasionally shuffling out of the way to let somebody get to the toilet.

You snap out of your trance as the train screams into your stop. Once, this station held so much promise. It was the starting point for nights out with mates, carrying you on towards the carefree mistakes of your teenage years.

Now, it's the last line of defence for the lie you've created.

As soon as you step outside those doors and meet your dad, waiting patiently in the car park, it might all come tumbling down.

The train doors shut behind you and it rolls away. Grab your case and head for the exit.

F FOR FAIL

I got my grade today and it's F, for you've failed; but I
read it as I'm fucked, for this is a pebble atop the
mountain of gravel I hide from my parental help for
shame. That I know all they want is for me to do well
but I can't do well, I can't even do okay, okay would be a
dream. A beautiful slumber picture show of an F
morphing into a C to B to an A; but I have to wake into a
nightmare no matter how long I wait in my dream, I
wake again to being me, holding a banner stamped with
an F.

The train journey home lasts at least an eternity but I get there eventually and through the window I see my dad waiting to hear about my day and I want to tell him but I can feel the impending lie building in my body as I cross the threshold from cold outside to freezing shelter.

The door closes behind me with a prison click and he greets me like a friend, he is, but in that moment he is more my warden, my heart breaks and I see in his eyes he does the same when I give him my best grin and tell him "everything is great" but beg him not to go online and find the F that tells him "your son lies"

I am found out as I always am. Dreading the speeches and the stop-think-and-make-a-plan, these words that once burned into my soul are a record I've played too much, a song that used to touch me; so deeply, has started to warp and crack to the point it's just water off a feathered back. And all I see is the red ink, skyscraper F always telling me I'm fucked.

I have to switch lanes. No, more than that, change cars, to do what I love instead of what people would love for me to do. It's really the simplest thing when I'm happy at the hardest point of what I want instead of miserable before I even begin to limp after attempting the sensible thing. But that F; that told me to leave, that I was not welcome nor cut out to persist. That I was fucked. I have been pushed to say the two words to leave the nightmare and find my bliss: fuck this.

The wind leaks through the doors as they slide open to let people out. It snakes through the crowds and bites at your soggy trouser cuffs. Ignore the wet sting in your shins as you slope through the hordes, sidestepping out of the way of people making a beeline for the platform or an overpriced, bitter cup of coffee.

The rush of air keeps pushing back as you get closer to the doors. You wish you could just drop your bag and let it take you. Float off into nowhere and be forgotten instead of facing things. But you can't. The doors slide back and you step out into the crisp winter afternoon.

The front of the station is a conveyor belt of people hopping in and out cars. You scan through the crowd as people flash past your face and shove their way to the front doors. You're pushing against the current and you can feel the frustration push past you, the only person standing stationary in front of the entrance.

You can't see him, maybe he's forgotten. You know that he wouldn't, but you can hope for a moment. A walk home would give you another half hour at least.

Right now, a version of you exists in their mind- a better version, one that they could be proud of. Instead, their damp son wheels his case of filthy clothes across the car park, a deflated parody of the boy who left home all those months ago.

After a few moments, you spot the number plate. You couldn't recite it if you were asked, but you recognise it instantly. You saw it on your way out of the house every day for years. The case rattles over the gravel and a fine dust bursts up, caking your sodden trousers as you cross the car park.

He spots you in the mirror and turns around as you approach the back of the car. Chuck your bag in the boot and open the door. Climb in and muster the best smile you can. He looks so glad to see you.

"How's it going, train alright?"

"Yeah, good. Busy."

Yawn. Explain the early morning, couldn't get any sleep on the train. Not a free seat in the whole thing. He rattles on about the state of the train service, you nod in agreement as he pulls out of the car park and along the high street.

There's only so far this conversation can go.

Sooner or later, he'll start asking harder questions. Ones that require better lies. But it's ok, you're well practised. You've mastered the art of being vague enough to be convincing.

"Anyway, how's it all going?"
"Alright, yeah."

Throw another yawn in there, fend off any more questions. Rest your head against the window and lean into the rumble of the road. Shut your eyes for a second and imagine that you're anywhere else. Focus on the rhythmic roll of the wheels and feel it vibrate through your skull.

You've been silent for too long. Ask about everybody at home, that'll buy you some time. Zone out as he starts talking, detailing how well your brothers are doing, how much their own children have grown.

Meanwhile, memories rush by outside the window. Some things have changed completely, while others are like ghosts of a former life.

Newsagents have new signs, your favourite chippy does kebabs now. The park you and your mates used to piss about on has a new slide. It's on the edge of familiar and comforting, but it's also a reminder that everything has moved on. There's no way back.

You know every turn off by heart. Every movement of the wheel already plays out in your head before he reacts. The lights change to red.

Sit up and stretch your neck, nod along with a smile. You'll be stuck here for a while- these lights always take ages to change if you're turning right. Usually, it's annoying, but today, you don't mind.

As you look out of the window, you notice he's in a different lane. The lights switch and he pulls away, heading straight on. You crane your neck and look right, staring down a road you've walked a thousand times. The rumble of the car switches to an almost silent hum as he picks up speed on a brand-new stretch of road.

This used to be an empty field. As a teenager, you camped out here with some mates after somebody managed to sneak some beers.

Anxiety creeps up and you get a sudden urge to jump out of the car. This isn't the right way. You've gone past the road you know and it's disappearing into the distance behind you. He notices you looking back.

"They finished it a few months back. Much quicker this way"

You watch his hands on the wheel, count the junctions up ahead. Think about where home is. The road stretches ahead and winds around the corner. When is he going to turn?

In a year or two, the tarmac on the road will start to wear. Chunks will come out and the smooth surface will disappear.

The familiar rumble of the car will return, and you'll barely remember driving down the other way. But right now, all you want is to wind down that road under the shade of the trees.

Finally, he turns and you join back onto a familiar stretch. Unclench your fists, exhale, sit back. You could just tell him right now. Get it over with because he's going to find out anyway. Just turn around and say I fucked it all up- then wait for the consequences.

You know it'll be endless lectures and detailed plans about your future, hashed out over the dinner table while you sit idly by and wait to see what your fate is. You're never involved in the conversation, of course. Everybody else knows what's best for you, that's how you ended up here in the first place.

You're not far from home now. You look over as he slows at a junction and hits the indicator. It kicks into life and starts ticking, the orange light showing everybody that he knows exactly where he's going. He always has, so have the rest of them. But you just hit the open road and see where it goes without any semblance of direction. Just enjoy the drive and work out the destination along the way.

He pulls out of the junction and rounds the corner, not far from home. If you want to tell him, you haven't got much time left. Maybe it'll be easier if you do it now, while he's focused on the driving. You won't have any backup though, and you can't walk away from the inevitable lecture. You decide to wait. It'll happen eventually but why not make it a problem for another day?

Telling him won't get you anywhere anyway. It'll be the same conversation again, like a stuck record. Make the sensible choice, set yourself up for a career, check the boxes off the list.

But you've tried that and you're failing. Doing what everybody else would love you to do doesn't work. You need to do what you love to do.

He's fallen silent now, you're not giving him much and he's not going to press you. You've done a good job of convincing him you're tired.

The car rolls on as a light drizzle starts running down the windscreen. The wipers screech into action and smear it over the glass, making the world outside a blur. Follow the drips down the window, peering through them and turning the world on its head. They slide down, changing course and winding their way to the bottom before disappearing. You wonder if that's how you'll end up, stumbling from one thing to another, pushed on by the breeze.

Would that really be so bad? Everybody else has pushed you this way and that, told you what you should be doing without a thought for what you wanted to be doing. Now you're trapped in this car, stewing in the atmosphere, trying to decide whether to be honest or just keep up with the endless lies.

Whatever you decide, you can't sit in this car, driving the same route over and over. You need to switch lanes and start focusing on what you want. Time is precious, and you're wasting it.

You're still absorbed in the raindrops on the window when you feel the slight lurch of the car coming to a halt. The handbrake crunches and the engine settles down. You look up as he gets out and heads for the front door. You've missed your chance to tell him now.

Get out and grab your case from the boot. You can feel the weight of your failures buried inside somewhere. You drag them along the driveway.

There's a wreath on the front door and you can see the tree glittering through the window. The whole house has that warmth over it as everybody prepares for an idyllic family Christmas. You hear them milling about inside, excited for your arrival. It only makes you feel more guilty.

You're welcomed with hugs and pats on the back as you drag your case and set it down at the bottom of the stairs. For a moment, you feel a slight sense of relief in the familiarity but it's not long before the weight of expectation rushes back.

With every happy greeting the anxiety builds. Everybody wants to hear all about how great you're doing. Tell them you just need to put your case upstairs.

Your feet sink into the carpet with each step, slowly wrapping around your damp socks. As you climb, it feels harder to pull your foot free and take the next step. There's familiarity here, but it's suffocating. At the top of the stairs, you see your bedroom door.

It's just how you left it. A little time capsule from a time you understood. The room is littered with relics from your childhood. Passing interests that never materialised into anything- a guitar, novelty sized rugby balls and a participation trophy from school.

Throw your case down and sit on the bed for a moment. You just need a breather. Take out your laptop and load it up. While it kicks itself into gear, look around the room.

How many nights did you spend in here, inventing stories in your head about the beginning of the rest of your life? The anticipation building towards that day when you cut yourself free and went out on your own. The endless possibilities and amazing experiences, all waiting there for you.

But even back then you knew, somewhere in the back of your mind, that you were setting yourself up for failure. It was never your choice to go to Uni, it was just another step that was decided for you.

You can hear them all downstairs, chatting and rushing around, preparing for a family Christmas that will ultimately be tainted by another disappointment of your making.

You hear a knock at the door and mum calls through from the other side.

"Everything ok?"
"Yeah. Just sorting stuff out."

She pushes the door open and reaches round with a cup of tea. She sets it on the side and smiles. She's just happy to have you home. You can barely talk to anybody because your head is filled with the big fat 'F 'scrawled on your life now.

The way that she edges into the room suggests that they've all been discussing you downstairs. Mum says you seem off, dad reassures her you're just tired, even though he sees it too.

"Are you coming down?"
"Yeah, just sorting my bags."

She smiles again and closes the door. You look over at your laptop and open your grades. Scroll through the pages of classes that you barely understand or care about. The endless stream of fail, fail, fail. Your heart starts thumping as you put yourself in the mind of your dad, looking back at you with that look he does.

Imagine the crisis meeting called to help you sort your life out and work out where you're going. What will they decide for you this time?

Slam the laptop shut and start pacing around the room, searching for some flash of inspiration. There must be something you're excited about. A thing that you can imagine doing day in, day out without losing your mind. You can't go into this fight unarmed. If you're going to bare all and start plotting your own course, you need a solid idea of where you're going.

They'll ask all the usual questions; How? Why? What if? They'll put that face on and tell you how nice it would be, but it's just not realistic.

The truth is, you don't need an end goal, you just need a feeling. A small thread to grab and pull on to see what unravels.

Maybe nothing happens and you try something else on for size. Failing at something you want is always better than succeeding at something you don't.

That big fat 'F', written across your head in aggressive red pen wouldn't be so hard to stomach if you were working towards something good. Because you don't always know what the future holds, and you don't know how many chances you're going to get. So don't keep wasting time like this.

Stop in the middle of the room and close your eyes. You're standing on a cliff edge, violent winds battering you as you struggle to keep your balance. The harsh rain whips your face and sharpens your mind.

For the first time in so long, you have clarity. The ocean looms below, raging at the rocks. Huge waves crash against the cliff and the dark waters swirl together. You don't know how deep it goes. You know that you'll be tossed around, and you'll have to fight hard to keep your head above water.

Your whole family stands behind you, begging you to turn back. Come back where it's safe, you don't know what's down there. You could sink and never come back.

It's true, the waves could take you as soon as you hit the water. No matter how hard you thrash and kick, you'll never get your head above the threshold again. Slowly but surely, you'll be dragged down to the bottom.

But you might not sink, you might swim. The sheer power of determination will carry you through as you glide through the water, weaving around the waves and riding them forward. Even if you do sink, you won't sit at the bottom for long. You can climb back to the top of the cliff and try again, and next time, you'll be ready.

You still hear them in the back of your mind, urging you to step back from the edge. They can show you another way around. You don't want another way around, though. They can't understand that right now, but one day they will.

Turn back for one last look, then face front. It's simple, one foot in front of the other. Let your first step hang over the edge, feel it sway in the wind. Enjoy being off balance for a few seconds before you push off and plunge towards the foaming waters below.

****

Open your eyes. Your body feels lighter. The tension in your back and shoulders is melting away and your jaw falls loose. You've forgotten this feeling.

Things have gone quiet downstairs. They're probably sitting in the living room, sipping at cups of tea and ignoring the tension. None of them want to mention the blindingly obvious fact that you're not there.

Maybe they all know why, but they're just hoping that it's not true. Everybody is silently praying that you'll come downstairs and tell them that everything is great, you're thriving, and you've found your calling. In a way, it's true, but not in the way that they imagine.

As you head down the stairs, the anxiety begins to resurface. You know what you need to do but you don't want to let them down. They won't understand because they always need a clear plan. It doesn't fit with their way of doing things and that scares them. You're terrified that they will be disappointed.

They will, for now. But things will change when your world is turned upside down. Any kind of plan will be ripped out from under you all. Priorities will be shifted and they'll start thinking about things differently when the harsh randomness of life can no longer be ignored.

You walk through into the living room and they fall silent. Mum gives you a smile and gestures for you to sit down. Everybody waits for a second.

Who's going to make the first move? Sip your tea and leave some space. You don't really know how to launch into this just yet.

Eventually, mum says -

"Come on then- How was your first term?"

That impulse to lie suddenly grabs you. You're back on that cliff, towards the water thinking, what the hell am I doing?

See how excited she is, desperately clinging onto this version of you that they've created in their own heads.

Feel the tension creep back into your shoulders, your teeth scrape together as your jaw tightens.

It's there in your throat, the truth, but it's stuck. The internal argument starts raging. You could just lie, say it's all fine.

Work out what to do later and avoid all the disappointment. But it's killing you, you can't keep on like this. Is it worth all the upset just so you can jump off the cliff edge with no idea where you're going?

Stop. Breathe. Think. This all seems so big right now but it's not. All you have to do is tell them. Step forward and let yourself fall.

"Actually, there's something I need to tell you.

A MOUSE AMONG GIANTS

All around I see those that love me, mine the rocks of my failures and shortcomings in the hope that they will unearth a single gem of pride to be held amongst the millions sprung from previous quarries. It is my crushing knowledge that they will search forever and never retrieve that which I cannot provide.

I have been raised upon the shoulders of titans and told that makes me one among them, until the sharp realisation I find now that I have fallen from great heights, is that a shared name is not a shared worth and to count myself equal of mine would be an insult to their well-earned title.

In light of this, a departure is far more than appropriate and would be gratefully executed would it not be for the fear of bringing these gods around me to their knees with a selfish final act.

All there is left is the possibility that a random act may carry my shame away from the mighty pack that I stain, and hope that such an act may occur before I fail them once again.

Until then I remain a mouse among giants.

The room bustles with laughter and stories. But despite the festival of conversation wrapped around you, your eyes remain fixed on the picture of you and your brothers hanging on the wall above the armchair.

Arms are wrapped around each other, the familiar family smile plastered across each of your faces. A draping of tinsel tumbles and curves around the frame, blocking you from the picture.

On the seat below, Granny sits rocking slightly with a sherry-fuelled - how much they've grown smile - on her face. The fire and flurry that is Christmas has settled down now, and you all stew in the post-dinner glow, nursing drinks and stomachs on the sofa.

You woke up feeling rough after last night, and it's been a cocktail of drinks since then. Despite the heavy days, you still don't feel drunk.

In fact, your pretty sure it's impossible to get drunk on Christmas. The sheer weight of the holidays in your belly soaks up every beer you throw at it, bloating you and everyone else in the room. But no doubt you'll still try.

Granny yawns and her eyelids sink behind thick rimmed glasses. Then your dad yawns. A little after, you yawn.

Christ, you hadn't realised how tired you were until now. And not just full belly tired; it's like every muscle aches as you lift the bottle to your lips.

It's been like this the whole time you've been home. Every family moment or beer with friends has left you feeling empty, like you were dead weight noosed around the people and streets you once called home.

Each second dragged you closer to this sofa, this celebration, this moment. The people you love surround you, curious about your time away, but tip toeing around the fact that after this celebration is over, you'll be a dropout and nothing more.

"Isn't that right?"

Shit, for the millionth time tonight you forgot to listen. Nod your head and smile, then hide any necessary response behind another swig of beer.

Your uncle turns back to your brother, sitting on the other side of the sofa. The two of them quietly sip at a whiskey. Your uncle gesticulates with his free hand, the sleeve of a Christmas jumper slipping to show the gleam of a new watch- a present to himself, as he calls it.

Another one of his theories whistles over you and your brother's heads. Something about manufacturing shortcuts and fussy craftsmen. Nothing bad really, just boring.

Your brother manages to catch your eye. Grin and flash him a little shrug.

"I'm telling you, never buy Italian. Nothing but trouble with that Alfa Romeo of hers."

He nods his head to your aunt on the other sofa, deep in conversation with mum and dad. Your brother is straight up staring at you, with a look that says, could you help me out here.

He swirls his whiskey in the glass and takes a short draw of it. You turn to the table where your own empty glass is, shot down in one.

You take the last sip of your beer and roll your stomach to the edge of the sofa.

"Anyone want a drink?"

Your uncle declines but your brother hands his glass over. Look around the room, everyone else happily tucked in their little conversations, granny asleep in the corner and the same drunk-red smile on every face.

You take two steps to the door before...

"Oh love, while you're up."

Mum holds her empty glass of prosecco in the air. You take it and flash her a little smile. She thanks you and drops back into the sofa. Dad nods his head at you.

"There's a black box on the kitchen counter. Bring that through with you."

Nod and exit before any more orders come through.

Your feet slide along the wood flooring, the boards straining under the weight of the holidays.

The kitchen looks like a food bomb has dropped, every inch of counter scattered with serving platters, half empty drinks and cold leftovers. You finger a scrap of beef poking from under the tinfoil. Chew and pick until you hit gristle, spit it in your hand and toss it on a stray plate.

Lean against the counter and take a deep breath. As the rich kitchen air hits your lungs, the growling in your stomach starts to go, your body crying for a little help.

You need something to settle the booze down. Well, water would be a good start. You know that and come to think of it, you haven't had a single drop the whole time you've been home.

Yeah, water is what you need, you think as you open the fridge and crack into another beer. Hold the bottle high and take half down in a single mouthful. A burp rises from deep in your body and the day's festivities rushes into your mouth.

Prosecco. Chocolate. Crisps. Brussel Sprouts. Beer. Whiskey. Parsnips. Trifle. Beef.

The taste dwells on your tongue as a sharp pang of acid crawls up your throat. Your hand drops to the counter as you grimace and swallow it back down.

Open your eyes as a slow body shuffles in behind you.

"Alright love."

Granny shuffles into the kitchen and pauses to look at you with a smile. She's no longer the spritely woman from your memories. That person has slowly faded away, wrinkled and bent into a distant place in your mind. But like your dad always says, folk back then were built strong as ox's.

"Think I'll take a tea to bed."

She slides toward the kettle. You raise a hand to stop her.

"I'll make it. Take a seat."

You flick the kettle to life as she lowers herself in the soft chair at the head of the table. After a moment's search, you find her a mug from the back of a cupboard and toss one of her special Earl Greys in.

She sits there, content in the roaring silence of the kettle. It's not like the rest of them and their million questions about what went wrong and what you will do now.

While they've spent the whole day pretending to be interested in your half-responses and vague plans, she's just happy to see you healthy.

"It's been a lovely day, hasn't it?"
"Yeah. Great to see everyone again."

She rests a weary hand on the table, her fingers a little more curved with every passing Christmas. Her thumb slowly turns an ancient wedding ring over a wrinkled knuckle. As the water rumbles to a boil, she sighs deeper into the seat.

"Aye. And such a lovely dinner."
"They really pulled out all the stops, hey?"

Click and lift the rumbling kettle. The water steams into the cup. Fill it just above half and stir in a teaspoon of sugar. Lay the drink in front of her with the teabag still in, just the way she likes it.

"You alright getting this to the room?"
"Oh, I'll be fine. Thank you love."

She strains out of the seat, plants a kiss on your cheek and waddles out the door and to bed.

Suck down the rest of your beer and open another. Pour a whiskey for your brother and a prosecco for mum. On your way out, stop to slip the tiny black box on the counter in your back pocket.

"Just the person who will know..."

Mum announces you into the room, the whole sofa she's on staring at you divvy the drinks out. She pats the arm of the seat and you sit with an uncomfortable lean.

"Your aunt reckons right..."

They giggle to themselves. The huge grins on their faces make them look younger somehow, like they should be in a picture frame high on the wall somewhere.

"What's that then?"
"She reckons that a horse..."

More laughter. They fall into each other as they crease over, your aunt's chuckle turning into a smoky cough. Dad rolls his eyes at them and turns to you.

"Did you bring that box?"

You fumble your drink to the table and scramble the small black box out your pocket. Your oldest brother walks into the room and drops into the armchair.

"Oh perfect!"

Mum snatches the box from you and springs up a little too quickly. Her arms wave for balance and you reach out to catch her.

"Oh, mum's had a few."
"I'm fine thank you. Right everyone, who's ready for charades?"

There's a collective groan from you and your brothers. Your uncle lays down his empty glass and moves to the edge of his seat. Dad mirrors him and they eye each other up, a decades old sibling rivalry sparked in an instant.

Mum draws a small deck of black cards and starts to shuffle the deck. Her hands move almost sober as she ripples the cards together and stands in front of the log fire on the TV screen.

"Right, I'm first. Every man for himself."

She draws one and thinks for a moment, scrunching her lips and brow together. The card bends in her hand, she fans her face with it before leaning over and laying it face down on the table.

"Ok..."

She cranks the wheel of an old camera.
"It's a film."

She nods her head and pauses, tentatively cracking open the spine of...

"...and a book."

Mum nods, but she's not as sure about it. In her head she counts out 1,2,3...

"...four words."

"...fourth word is..."

Holding something invisible in her hand, she slowly brings it nearer and further her face. A magnifying glass maybe? Silence...

"Sherlock Holmes?"

Not quite. A slight pause to think, then she holds some invisible sheet in front of her face. She peers over the top of it, shifting her eyes from side to side.

"Oh, uh...Is it Pink Panther?"

Her fingers curl together. So close yet not quite the one. She shakes her head and tugs her earlobe.

"Sounds like..."

A finger juts towards her...

"Eye. Eye, oh. Spy!"
Mum points at your uncle with one hand and taps her nose with the other. He beams across the room, first round to him. Dad shakes his head and sighs.
Mum puts a hand on her hips as she mulls over the next clue. She raises three fingers.

"Third word..."

Out of nowhere, she stands straight as a pole, arms fixed to her side. Her right hand swings up and freezes at her brow in a firm salute...

"Army something...er, army inspector. NO, it's er..."

Your brother trails off...
The room is silent.

"Tinker, tailor, soldier, spy."

The words surprise you. They surprise everyone. Mum's
face lights up as she claps her hands together.

"YES!"

She skips back to the sofa and ruffles your hair. Dad pats
your back with a heavy hand, the proudest gesture he's
mustered the whole of the holiday. You take a heavy swig of
beer. The room goes silent and they all stare at you.
Fuck, you know what comes next.
Your uncles slaps his hands together and nudges your
brother.

Here we go then...

All you have to do is stand up. Stand up and draw a card.
Read the words and act them out. You don't even need to
speak. That's the point.
But the muscles in your legs refuse to move, your arms
chained to the bottle. The walls seem to drop away, the space
between you and the rest of the world stretches into
nothingness.
The lights dim and you're beckoned to the spotlight at the
centre of the room. This may be the greatest performance of
the evening.
Do you have it in you? The one man showing of - everything
is alright and I'm having a good time?

"Come on then..."

Don't think about it. Get up.
Something in your belly rumbles as you rock to your feet.
Each step churns the liquor through your head, waves of
Dutch courage spinning a half-dozen eyes around the room.

Get it together. Stand straight and draw a card. Walk yourself over to the centre of the room and puff out your chest. Own the moment, the space around you. Lie like you always do.

"Right then."

The card shakes in your hand. You can't remember if it's a film or not. It probably is, it feels like something they'd make into a film, but you haven't seen it. You count the words in your head which takes longer than you'd care to admit.

Christ, it reminds you of being a child again, standing in this very spot, the same faces staring back at you. Hair was thicker and darker, faces brighter. Granny would still be awake, there in the same armchair, leaning bright eyed into the game.

"Let me think."

Are you not still that same child? Have you really come any further than you were then, standing with all the clues in hand but incapable of doing anything about it?

"Come on, I'm falling asleep here."
"Alright. Alright."

Hold your hand in the air and count out…
Four words…
A book…
And a film.

Pause to gather yourself. Put a smile on your face so they don't notice your knee shuddering. An invisible hand grips at your throat and you struggle to breathe. If you keep the card in your hands, they'll notice it shake, so put it down.

"Right."

You want the world to stop. Not to go away, not to be different, you just want it all to stop. You need the world to be empty; an infinity of time for you to find the nothing and everything that you are so desperate for.

Instead, you reach for the beer, finish it in a swig and clap your hands together. Taking the floor again you hold out your hand and...

"Second word..."

Pucker your face and stick out your front teeth. Raise your clenched hands under your chin and sniff the air.

"Rats. Eh, Bunny."
"Oh Oh, Bunny boiler."
"That's not a film mum."
"Is it not?"
"You sure it's not a rat?"
"Mouse hunt...wait a book as well, right?"
"Diary of a wimpy kid."

The room erupts in laughter. Drop your arms and face and sigh. Mum catches the prosecco falling out her mouth. She swallows and splits the room with a howl of laughter.

Your uncle furrows his bushy eyebrows and clears his throat. He looks at you very matter of factly.

"Is it Mouse?"

Tap your nose and give him a wink. Take a deep breath as the room settles down. Raise your hand again...

"Fourth word..."

This one's easy. No need for anything really, just spread
your arms. Raise them up and down as if you were showing off
a new suit. Point at your uncle, both brothers and your dad.
Finally shove a thumb in your own chest and nod your head.

"The mouse and his child."
"I think that's before their time dear."
"Really?"
"The mouse in the house?"
"Stuart little."
"Ratatouille"
"Adventures of rat boy."

Shake your head. NO NO NO. Wrong.
Drop your shoulders and sigh, it should be obvious. Point at
your mum, then at your auntie while shaking your head. Puff
out your chest and give it a firm slap with both hands.
Silence.
From across the room, the stray ribbon of tinsel falls from
the picture on the wall. Your own face stares back at you,
younger and happier than you could ever imagine being again.
In the frame, your arm hangs across the shoulder of your
brother and you lean on him for support. The three of you are
beaming. A perfect holiday moment. A happiness you could
never know, one that only becomes more perfect with each
passing moment to oblivion.
You look down at yourself and you are that child again.
Four foot high and stood in front of the familiar faces of your
family.
The hand around your throat grips tighter. Lift your small
soft hands to your face. Through the gaps in your fingers, you
see the corner of your mum's mouth turn with a hint of
concern.

"Come on. Is it not obvious?"

You spread out your arms. From deep inside, a familiar childish voice calls out. He cries and screams at every aching fibre of your body, to the deepest void and crevice of your mind - what even am I?

"No one?"

The room is cold and silent. Your brother hears the small clink in your throat, like he is the only one that can sense that voice crying out inside of you. He sits upright and lays down his whiskey. Your eyes lock across the room.

For that moment, he sees right through the great Christmas performance to find a tiny morsel of a person scrambling in the dark. Something in his mind twigs and he smiles.

The air in your lungs escapes and the room falls away from you. Your brother slaps his hands together, stands and puts his hands in the air in celebration.

All eyes in the room turn away from the tiny shell of a person and focus on him. A wave of calm settles over your body as he looks at the fragment of a man and in the middle of the room.

He cuts through the awkward silence, with four words. A book. And (maybe) a film.

"Of Mice and Men."

PART II

I can see everybody else, gliding through the water while I'm moving backwards.

You're not moving backwards, you're just reaching for the wrong things.

What should I be reaching for?

Nothing. You've already caught it, you just don't see that right now. You used others as a mirror and that blinded you. But soon, you'll find your real self.

POETRY SLAM

I'm never going to change the world with my words.

I'm just another sheep amongst the Homo Erectus herds and who ever heard of a maverick in the flock achieve greater than a 200-volt shock from his collar.

I bleat my submission, surrender my idyllic fantasies and fall in line with the rest suffering from the human condition.

Hell, I'm only young so I will lash down my tongue.

*As much as I wish I could call to the masses, I can't even
hold the attention of the stranger that passes.*

*When did the common confidence deplete and true
leaders head to the retirement suite to chill and dope on
the self-doubt pill we are all addicted to.*

*Now I got the stage to release my pressure gauge.
I don't really know what to shout,
and I got this voice telling me I have nothing important
to talk about,
telling me I should run out.
It tells me there is no oasis to be found,
just failure, waste and drought…*

*I guess I'm just done with pen vs. sword,
On paper we are ignored so I'm gonna make the choice to
lock n' load my voice, fire off a round and hear that heart
stopping sound.
Grab my chance and let the poetry flow defend me from
the hordes that besiege my Alamo.*

*That's it, I'm doing this for the sheer bliss of escaping
the silent nothingness, of being told to stop and to sit
and my poems are a pile of shit.*

*So I, like the rest, am here to put my ramblings to the
test and just maybe change my own world for the best*

Front and centre, a tall bony figure with a ponytail
approaches the microphone and smiles through roll-up teeth.
From the back of the venue, the black backdrop and fairy
lights give the stage dim edges, making him float above the
crowd.

He thanks the audience and poets for making this evening possible.

Twenty or so bodies pack between the tight aisles, shuffled into the tiny back room at a pub. Despite the abundance of empty seats, the hum of the microphone and the tight ceiling make the room claustrophobic.

Anxious poets twitch in the crowd, hiding their nerves in the crushed and twisted cans of Red Stripe. A couple of them fold and re-fold lines scrawled across pages of A4. But most of them are like yourself, constantly checking their phones to reassure themselves that their poem still exists.

Open your own contribution to the collective anxiety. The words you've recited in your head a thousand times stare back at you, familiar phrases appearing as meaningless symbols in some strange new language. Lock your phone and tuck it back in your pocket, just two more to go, then you're up.

Turn to your brother, squirming in the seat beside you. His beer is warm and the chair juts at a funny angle into his back. So does yours, but your body is too tense to register anything right now.

The most you are capable of is the shuddering knee which vibrates through the sticky wood floor to another shuddering knee somewhere. The whole place slowly vibrates as everybody waits their turn.

Another scrawny writer is welcomed to the stage, a damp ripple of applause drags him into the spotlight. He mumbles his thanks and brushes a strand of dense blonde hair behind his ear.

It's hard to remember the poem that follows.

The mumbled words fall to the floor and roll between the legs of the crowd. By the time they reach the two of you at the back, they've lost all momentum and pool underneath the chair, asking quietly to be heard.

Every so often, a single line cuts through the puddle and leaps from the water, catching you off-guard. But for the most part, you and the rest of the crowd watch a man on stage, drowning in his words.

He rounds out the poem, hammering the same sentence over and over. On the fourth rotation, your brother leans in and asks if you fancy another. Nod and finish the can in your hand.

He slides from the metal chair and scrapes past chairs to the tiny bar at the back. Watch him while he stands at the bar, tenner in hand, trying to catch the attention of a disinterested barman.

If it wasn't for him, you wouldn't be doing this. These words hiding in your phone would still exist, and this man would still repeat himself, but you wouldn't be here in this stiff chair.

It really did happen by mistake, like most things that come about after another night in the local. Most of the regulars had emptied out of the place, leaving you two and a handful of diehards behind locked doors and heavy curtains. The landlord, a heavily tattooed bald man in a Santa hat poured the last pint for every straggler left behind.

In the beer-soaked after-hours, the topic of you dropping out reared its head. Nobody ever asked too many questions about it, and you never wanted to be honest about how bad things got.

That night though, you delved into it further than you had before. Maybe he brought it up, maybe you did, it doesn't really matter. But it was then, in that drunk vulnerable moment you decided to tell your brother something that you had only ever admitted to yourself.

You told him you wrote poems.

It was just as much a shock to you as it was him. As he leaned back and crossed his arms, you could tell he was trying to suss out if you were taking the piss or not.

The words sat just as uneasy in your own head. A poet. Instantly makes you think of dreary guys with long hair who smoke roll-ups; or the intolerable wankers at house parties who try too hard to be that guy.

But not you. You weren't even sure if they were poems, or what the point of them was. Before tonight, they were just somewhere to throw your thoughts. Cheaper than a therapist and a lot less commitment.

When you opened your phone and showed him a glimpse inside your head, it felt like a dam had burst. There were no tears, nothing overly emotional - just you reading your brother a poem in the local.

A pause... His smile...

He encouraged you to do something with them. That was the first time you ever thought of them as having purpose.

The ripple of hands brings you back to the room. The lanky guy on stage bows a little and thanks everyone. You slap your hand on your thigh and look around the crowd. For a second, you feel confident about tonight.

A chair scrapes through the settling quiet of the room. A couple rows ahead of you, a lone woman stands, grabs her jacket and rushes to the exit. Your eyes lock in the darkness at the edge of the crowd. There is a familiar feeling in her distant stare. A streak of light edges into the room as she opens the door and exits. The fear sneaks back in, resting in your gut and crawling up into your chest.

Your brother slides back into his seat and hands you a lukewarm can. You murmur thanks as the guy with a ponytail takes the stage again. He pauses for a moment, thanks the poet, then he thanks us. He pulls a list from his pocket and reads the next name aloud.

Last one and then it's you. You take a deep breath, your leg shaking to the point where people in front are turning around to glare.

He repeats the name, shielding his eyes and scanning the crowd.

Silence. The whole place pauses, curious eyes twitching through the rows. Hushed murmurs and discreet nudges. Who's the coward among us?

"Anyone? No?
    Next up is…"

Shit, it's you.

A smatter of applause bounces around the place. Your brother nods his head and claps the loudest. As you stand, the room doubles in size.

Every outline in the shadows bears two shining white eyes, all fixed on your nervous path between the aisles.

Somewhere between your chair and the stage, a familiar fear swells from your gut and drips all the way down to your fingers and toes. Well, it's more of a question really.

What if they all just think you're shit?

The thought of a silent response doesn't bother you. In fact, you'd welcome their indifference. But what if you are so bad, they actively chase you off the stage?

You decide that if things go that wrong while you're up there, you'll just repeat the last line five or six times. They seem to love that.

As you reach the bottom of the short set of steps, the feeling of inertia crumbles away, leaving your head floating above the room. The black void of the stage swallows you.

Stop and turn into the spotlight. It shimmers and sears your eyes, the hum from the speaker deafens you to everything but your pulse. It shudders and skips, settles, and starts to race.

The nerves crawl up your throat and lodge themselves there. With each breath your chest swells, the rush of air turning your gut and squeezing the veins in your neck.

Between you and the microphone, a small voice emerges inside the feedback from the speaker. As it garbles noises in the static, your eyes adjust to the faces hidden in the dark and shadowy crowd, a collection of grins staring back at you.

And still the voice goes on. Through the distortion it starts to chant something familiar. Here you stand on the edge of yet another cliff, looking deep into the void, a raspy voice calling your name.

The sound of words trapped in the back of the throat spreads through air and settles in the growling microphone as you lean in.

Smile and toast the beer to the audience. Thank them for having you. Compliments to everyone who read so far. You sound casual, almost confident as you drop a hand in your pocket.

You introduce yourself as a poet. The word lingers there for a while as you dig the phone out. In the pause, you swear you hear a murmur from somewhere in the darkness.

It's not until the light of your phone screen hits you that you realise how much your hand is shaking. The words shudder and buzz in front of your eyes. Tense your arm and try hold things steady, just long enough to read the first line.

The familiar words take on a new life altogether as you stare at the page. They remind you of something, a moment filed away as unimportant until right now.

This was the poem that started everything.

Sure, you'd written the odd note to yourself before and never thought about them again. But it was something in these lines that never left you. A feeling that drew you back into these pages long after the initial rush of the idea had faded.

After months of tweaking sentences, dropping and replacing words the realisation of what you were doing eventually came. You remember being alone in your room at Halls, an essay quietly ignored on the desk. As you read these words for the hundredth time a thought struck you.

Fuck. This is a poem.

It became easier from then. As soon as you realised this, each line and phrase beamed with new life. They became vessels for your tired body, able to detach you from reality for a single moment and suspend you elsewhere.

Not always a better place, but somewhere you could control.

Sometimes, you wonder if these words are even yours to begin with. It's hard to remember the version of yourself that wrote them, or what is left of him within you.

But on the stage, all that crumbles away. For the first time, these words are only accountable to you. It's your name being whispered, your tongue between the page and the crowd.

Last chance. If you want to back out, now is the time. Just lock your phone and leave the stage. Exit via the back door and join the panic attack of terrified poets outside.

See everything changes from here. Constantly and always, each moment folding and crashing you from one memory to the next. Nothing ever certain and nothing forever.

But we both know what follows. Two words cut through the microphone. Pause to give the title time to settle in their ears.

"Golden Moment."

A shimmer of applause. Take a final swig of beer and rest the can on the ground. Clear your throat and take a deep breath. Now the hard part.

The first line streams from the page, builds in your chest and escapes in a confident voice you barely recognise. You follow it into the unknown.

In the blinding light, surrounded by a sea of dim faces, you try to remember the version of you that first wrote these lines. The image is shaky, but he is probably alone in the dying hours of the night. He is awake still, he never sleeps.

The room is dark except for the piercing blue light held inches from his face. Thumbs race across the screen as he throws everything he has at the blank page.

That was once all you were, but since dropping out of Uni, you felt some part of that person fade into the background, appearing only in the words in front of you.

You still feel his uneasiness. The isolation and unbearable weight of direction are yours also. In almost every way, you two are the same; except for one thing, a hopeful thought lapping in the waves of light around you.

You think this might just work out.

With each new stanza, every line and flourish, you relax. Shoulders ease as your hand dips in your back pocket. Your feet pull from the stage, unstuck from under your rigid body. Your past self longed to disappear and the idea of being seen so clearly was terrifying. But now you're surprised how natural it feels to be under the glare of that spotlight.

Lifting your eyes into the crowd, you catch a glimmer of that past self, trapped in a darkness of his own creation. His face is the only one lit inside the audience, staring vacantly into his phone screen.

He mouths the next line with you.

"...I fear that regret may walk hand in hand with my freedom."

It is the first time you properly hear those words. You remember how real the pressure of it all felt in that moment. Now, it doesn't feel as heavy.

The image of your former self stares back at you from the crowd. The corners of his mouth curl, the screen clicks off.

Once again you are alone. But the fact is, you are on stage looking out. He is buried in this poem, looking in. Nothing can ever change that now.

As you push on, you don't feel as lost.

For once, you don't really feel much of anything, save for the heat of the spotlight on your face. You decide that, at least for the moment, you are happy here.

The poem draws to a close. You raise your eyes to the crowd, puff out your chest and unleash the finish. All the emotions, the weight of these words pour in ocean sized waves at the crowd. The final line echoes between them -

"Then this time, is the chronological tomb of my splendour..."

From inside the crowd, you catch sight of your brother's smile. He lifts his phone and takes a picture. With the last of your breath, expel the final remnants of your former self.

"...in solemn remembrance of my days in colour."

The space between the last word and first tentative clap drags on forever. A few more hands ripple out towards the back. And then there's your brother, making enough noise to fill every empty seat in the place.

The crowd settles down before you even have time to get one foot off the stage. Ponytail is right up there, thanking you and lining up the next poet.

An odd sense of calm settles over you as you walk through the rows. Every set of eyes ignores you- they're all fixed firmly on the next person shaking on the stage. You can't decide if you were expecting more or less of a reaction from them. But it doesn't matter.

It's hard to feel anything other than the glow of that light pulsing down upon you still. You hope this feeling is big enough to carry you through the rest of the night. Hell, this could probably do you for the week.

Apologise your way between the narrow rows and drop into the chair. You can't get rid of the embarrassed smile on your face. Your brother gets a firm hand on your shoulder and smiles, the same smile as that first time in the pub.

"That was great."

He raises his beer.

"Honestly man, well done."
"Thanks"

You exhale and slump into the hard metal.

You want to tell him everything; each feeling that raced through you, how empty your mind was yet still so alive with thought. But you don't. The moment passes and quietly slips into the next performance.

You both turn to the stage, your brother sips at his beer. In the calm shadow of the crowd, you let yourself relax for the first time all night.

You don't take in a single word from the stage. Your mind chugs along and picks up speed. The whole night had led up to that moment and now it's behind you, a sea of possibilities has opened. For the first time, that excites you.

Tomorrow, you will apply for that job dad showed you. Maybe he's right, maybe it's the best thing for now. You will print out a pile of CV's and plaster them about town. You will save up money and move out of your parents again. You will write another poem to shadow this one.

Your fingers twitch at the idea of it. Take out your phone and open a new page. In the darkness at the back of the room, you capture the new version of yourself in a single line -

I'm only young so I will lash down my tongue.

Bury your phone and try to pull your focus back into the room. In the corner of your eye, your brother checks the time and takes a big swig of beer.

It's getting on now and you've both got a long way back. He'll go to his and you to mum and dad's. You'll message a bit about tonight, but it'll be a while before you see him again.

You want to thank him, to let him know how grateful you are for forcing the poems out from the darkest parts of your mind and into the light.

Who knows where you'd be otherwise.

Reaching under the seat, your hand searches for a beer that isn't there. As the poet on stage finishes his verse, you sigh and drop back into your chair.

The room fills with applause. Your brother leans over to you.

"That last one was brilliant."

You nod along, though you didn't catch a single word of it.

The poet steps over your beer and leaves the stage with the same proud smile you had plastered across their face. They smile at the group of friends waiting for them back in the seats.

Ponytail calls for a quick break to refresh drinks and chain cigarettes.

And the whole time you sit there, wondering whether to go back up and collect what you left on the stage.

You decide against it, turn to your brother and offer him a drink.

MYSTERY

*My future is a mystery, there's fog on the path, but bless
my eyes with foresight and what would I see: a man
made in the millions, cruising Bondi Beach, driving
flashy cars, money growing on the trees... Unlikely.*

*The lights are off, my compass doesn't point north, I'm
lost but free. Friends, family, family friends all know
what's best for me, each with a secret – how to succeed -
don't get me wrong, I'm grateful but this is my journey.*

*Maybe I'm a poet in an attic flat, never got much money,
wallet on the floor, empty. Diet of ready meals and Aldi
deals. Now that would be the dream if not for a lack in
luxury.*

*The lights are off, my compass doesn't point north, I'm
lost but free. Friends, family, family friends all know
what's best for me, each with a secret – how to succeed -
don't get me wrong, I'm grateful but this is my journey.*

*I could live with each or none of the above, knowing
what I want to do is just too tough, I could be in the Gobi
or lost at sea. I don't know but in the meantime on with
the show.*

The beer hits the bottom of the glass and ricochets up the
sides. It slides back down and settles, leaving a residue of tiny
bursting bubbles. You watch it, hypnotised as the level slowly
rises towards the top.

Behind you, the evening is in full swing. The room is filled
with the low hum of forced, polite conversation. After a few
more rounds, it will loosen into raucous laughter or awkward
honesty that is regretted in the morning. It's not the kind of
place you'd choose to come to.

Turn back to the bar as the head hits the precipice of the
glass and the barman flicks the tap off. He puts it on your tray
with two glasses of red and a gin and tonic. You stand for a
second, scanning the tables and racking your brains. He sighs
at you and points to the table in the far corner.

You edge slowly through the crowded room, haphazardly
balancing the tray without a hint of grace. The other waiters
dip in and out of tables with a smile, putting glasses down and
disappearing without a beat. They move unnoticed while you
draw frowns and tuts as people shunt their chairs in. Mouth a
quick sorry and give them an awkward smile.

Eventually, you reach the table and set the tray down. They
watch impatiently as you take the drinks off and set them
down in the centre.

The man at the other side makes a point of reaching over with his lobster-red forearm and taking his pint. How you've inconvenienced him. You try to put the glass of wine down while avoiding his hairy, sun-mottled arm.

His shirt is crisp white, open to reveal a flash of his tanned, leathery chest. The tie is sitting on the table in a crumpled heap. He leans in his chair, one arm cocked over the back, absorbing the false attention of the table.

The woman sat next to him stares into the distance as he rambles on. Clearly, she's heard it all before and it wasn't interesting the first ten times. She seems relieved when you arrive with the drinks and the conversation stops.

She looks younger than him, probably about ten years or so. You wonder if she's his wife, disappointed that the man she married has turned into a dull workaholic that barely pays her any notice. Maybe she'd leave if she had any idea where to go.

Although, you could be wrong. Behind closed doors he could be a kind, loving husband. You doubt it though.

Finish putting the drinks down and wish them a good evening. It goes ignored and the deafening silence at the table falls away as he launches back into whatever dull boast the rest of them were nodding along to before you arrived.

The fake leather of your new shoes digs into your heel with every step. The blister is already forming and you're only half an hour into your shift. By the end of the night, it'll be a raw mess, soaking into your sock.

You glance back at the table. Look at his shoes. They look pretty much the same as yours, but he paid a lot more for them. He's not getting blisters any time soon. The rest of the table are still locked into his one-man show, unable to get a word in.

You put the tray back on the bar and ask if any more drinks need taking. He looks up briefly, shaking his head before collapsing back into his phone.

After a few moments, he notices you out of the corner of his eye, lurking like a lost child.

"Erm, just head into the back and tidy up a bit."

You edge past him and head behind the bar into the back room. It's filled with empty barrels and cardboard litters the floor. You start picking up the boxes and ripping the seams open. Cram them into the recycling bin in the corner and look around for something else to do.

You spot a pile of champagne corks and the little metal wire bits from the top. You pull up a barrel and sit down. The wire from the cork bends and contorts in your fingers, easily moulded into whatever shape you like.

You play around with it, snapping it and twisting it back together. After a while, you end up with a delicately crafted sculpture of a jaded businessman with a failed marriage and six different sports cars.

You spend more time than you realise lost in the thin golden wire. Eventually, your boss pokes his head around the corner.

"What are you doing back here? There's drinks need taking."

Shit. Pocket it and tell him you were just having a sit-down. He shakes his head at you and mumbles something under his breath as you rush past him. Grab the tray and look back at him.

"Same as before."

Brilliant. Start making the journey across the crowded room. It's more treacherous this time, the drinks have been flowing for a bit. People are less aware of their chairs sticking out and they're too absorbed in their conversations to notice you loitering behind them, trying to catch their attention by doing nothing at all. You move behind an old woman as she reaches into her coat. The tray wobbles and splashes a mix of beer and wine onto the tray.

By the time you reach the table, it's dried into a sticky mess. One of the women gets up and goes heads for the door with a pack of fags as you set the tray down and prize the glasses away. He picks the pint up and examines it. You've short-changed him, but he won't say anything.

Another button has come down on his shirt and the carefully curated dusting of hair covering his sun-spotted head is starting to get out of control. He puts the drink down and leans back in his chair, gazing around the room while he waits for you to leave. The small metal model of him in your pocket digs into your leg.

You slip a hand in and roll it around as you walk from the table. You've captured the arrogant lean and the laid-back demeanour in wire form. As you get back to the bar, you pull it out and start tweaking it.

Accentuate the big belly, make the head a little messier. As you work, you wonder what this little golden man does. He oozes confidence and even in a place like this, you can tell he thinks he's top of the food chain.

He's the kind of guy that probably spends half the year at his beach front second home in Australia, cruising up and down in an embarrassing red convertible.

126

When he needs to work, he gets up at six in the morning and starts by reading the financial times with a strong coffee. He skips breakfast and then starts calling people to shout down the phone.

It's probably something to do with finance, but maybe he doesn't really know what's going on anymore. He's just the one people answer to when things go south.

After a morning of intimidation, he heads out for a game of golf to avoid spending time with his wife for as long as possible.

The day ends with the inevitable awkward dinner before she heads to bed, and he goes back to staring at emails and watching his bank balance.

Maybe he was a self-made man. His twenties were spent falling from job to job, just like you. But then he landed an entry level position and worked his way up to the top. It could happen to anybody.

You could end up like that one day. Everything would be easy if you were rich. But somehow, you don't see yourself in a place like this, boring a table of people that are probably only here because you're paying.

Your train of thought is interrupted when the barman comes back. You quickly cram the little golden financier in your pocket again and grab a cloth to look busy. It's an old trick and he's used it plenty of times himself.

"Can you grab some glasses from the kitchen?"

He gestures behind you to the swinging door with the little porthole. Waiters revolve in and out with steaming hot food and empty plates. The door swings violently as you push through and the heat and hiss smack you in the face.

The sound of frivolity from outside gets drowned out by curt instructions fired back and forth through the haze of smoke and grease.

Budge through to the back, tucking your elbows in as you go.

"Watch out."

A body juggling three plates rushes by as you move further into the kitchen. You see a young kid buried in the sink at the far end, can't be more than sixteen.

He grabs the plates, sprays them down, and throws them in the dishwasher at lightning speed. The robotic motion repeats over and over as he stares straight into the wall with a vacant look in his eyes. When the dishwasher is filled, he slams the top down and lets out a sigh.

He sees you coming and points to the tray of glasses balanced on the side. You thank him and he gives you a nod before heading out the back door. It opens into the car park and the cool evening air rushes into the kitchen for a second. The kid wipes his forehead with the back of his hand and grabs a tattered book from his back pocket. He sits hunched over on the curb and bends the book open, clutching it one hand and burying himself inside.

You wonder what he's reading as you grab the tray and make your way back out of the kitchen. You set them down on the side at the back of the bar and start putting them away.

The barman comes back and gives you a pat on the back.

"Cheers mate. Grab five minutes when you're done with that."

You rush to get the glasses done and then head into the back to grab a seat on an old barrel. You root around on the floor to find another piece of wire.

Start with the head, make it big. The kid seems like he's got a lot of ideas in there. Get the curve in the back to capture that intense concentration. Push a few bits of old box to the side and find one of the little foil bits. Fold it and flatten it to make the book.

You wonder what it was. Maybe a poetry book or some old beatnik novel that he wishes his mates would be interested in. An idea that he models himself after.

He was bored in school, found it too rigid. The teachers weren't interested in his ideas. So now he's here, washing up to get a bit of cash for now.

But his real passion is poetry. He spends his free time scrawling and sketching in notebooks, he doesn't like writing on a phone. He's not looking to be famous or anything, just as long as he's got enough cash for a dingy flat and some food in the fridge. You wonder if you'd be happy living like that.

You can't get the legs right. They keep coming out all twisted and unnatural. You check the time on your phone, it's time to get back out there. Put the poet kid in your pocket next to the financier and grab another champagne top before you head back to the bar.

Some of the tables have cleared out, others are in the process. The empty glasses and crumbs call out to you. The barman gives you a nod as you grab a spray bottle and cloth and head out there. As you absently wipe the tables clean and say goodnight to people that move past you towards the door, you spy the financier, sinking into his chair. Reach into your pocket and squash him a little.

Things wind down slowly over the next half an hour or so. People filter out, empty glasses are cleared and taken to the poet in the back. The financier and a couple of his remaining guests are the last to leave, pushing it all the way to the end. The staff rap fingers on the bar and busy themselves, glancing back at the table every five seconds.

You watch them as you help the slow clean up.

Eventually, you run out of things to pretend to do. Staff wander back and forth aimlessly, some head into the kitchen to help back there. You sit down on a stool, hidden by the bar. You reach into your pocket and set out your models on the shelf. There's one more champagne top in there. Maybe a self-portrait this time.

You start making the head and then turn your attention to the body. The first attempt stands tall and proud, with a sort of arrogance about it, but it's not right. Maybe it needs to be more subtle, maybe you should add a book like the other one.

It takes the financier another half an hour to finally finish up and ask for the bill. In that time, you bend the piece of wire into countless different people. Twisting and breaking it, reforming it and breaking it again. But never quite capturing yourself in it.

The barman comes through and tells you to take the bill over to the last table. You stumble through the confusing menu on the till and eventually manage to print it out. The financier waits impatiently, holding his card in the air. You take his small wire doppelgänger out of your pocket and bend the arm slightly, so it grips the receipt.

As you set it down on the table, he frowns at it and takes the bill, leaning back slightly to check it over. Hand him the card machine, wait in the uncomfortable silence. Thank him. Goodnight.

You walk away and look back as he picks up the figure and gently crushes himself, dropping the crumpled ball of wire back onto the table.

You're told to head into the back and help finish up in the kitchen, then you can all head home.

It's quiet in there now. The harsh heat and commotion from the grills and pans are gone, replaced by spray bottles and talk of takeaways on the way back. You head over to the poet at the back and start helping him unload the dishwasher.

"Thanks."
"No worries."

Not long later, the kitchen is spotless, ready for another assault tomorrow. Everybody says their goodbyes and you go to find your boss. He thanks you for a job well done, though you're not sure he's being totally honest. Take off the greasy apron and throw it in the box on the side on your way out.

Walking to the bus stop, the fatigue starts to kick in. The constant motion of the night has quietly died, and your body is beginning to ache. It's cold, but the goosebumps on your arms are welcome after the sweat of the kitchen and the back and forth to the tables all night.

The bus stop is empty, and you bask in the quiet, listening to the rumble of distant cars. It's a weird feeling. A sense of achievement mixed with a looming dread about next time. The whole façade gets exhausting, having to pretend that ferrying drinks to tables is the start of something and not just a stopgap.

The bus pulls up with just a few people on board. Everybody has already headed out for the night, and nobody is ready to come back yet. Sit near the back and close your eyes, half sleeping but never too deep that you miss your stop.

When you get off the bus and start walking towards home, you notice the pain in your heels for the first time. Every step drags rigid leather across the bare skin and skims another layer off.

Make the short hobble home and rummage around in your pocket for your keys, making sure to be quiet as you come in. Carefully prize the shoes off and inspect the damage. It'll be sore for days and you'll have to put them back on before it heals up.

Everybody is in bed, the house is quiet. You suddenly remember that you haven't eaten since lunchtime, so you go to the fridge and fix yourself a sandwich. Sitting in the dark, eating it, your bed calls to you.

Give the plate a quick rinse and creep up to bed. Your clothes land in a heap on the floor and the model of the poet tumbles out. Reach over for it and set it on the desk. Chuck your shirt out of the way and find the mangled failure of a self-portrait you attempted earlier.

Sleep doesn't come easily. Your body is exhausted but your mind is still whirring with drinks orders and the clink of empty glasses. The sandwich turns in your stomach.

You lay on your back, staring into the ceiling as you slowly unfurl the ball of wire and straighten it out, starting again from scratch.

Hours later, the sun creeps through the curtains as your heavy eyelids struggle under their own weight. All night you've been sculpting a thousand different people. Never sure of who you're going to make next.

As sleep finally comes, you straighten the wire once more and smile to yourself, safe in the knowledge that you can bend it into whoever you like.

WHAT I WANT TO BE

What do you want to do with your life? It seems people can't get enough of the sound of my total confusion and youthful loss of direction so since this question is too tough, I will substitute it for 'what do you want your life to be?'. Well for me, I want daft adventures with an ever changing back drop wrapped up in excitement, I want my life to be the Beano written by Tarentino, I want to go toe to toe with the whatever in the wherever.

Now I know this has been the dream for every starter adult from the loincloth clad cave dwellers wondering what's in the next valley to the Viking warriors long boating through the Baltic en route to rob an unsuspecting Brit to the new world bound explorer's galley; and yes I could, like the many my age, sub the world behind the glass for internet fast pics and blogs of those adventures already done but somehow that just seems less fun.

But here's the funny thing, with my plan to be fancy free, to make reality from a dream you need money, and that doesn't come easily, so really, to get what I want to be, I need to know what I can do, you can see how this is tricky when there is no calling for a highly paid procrastination guru.

Your eyes flit open and closed a few times and you're gripped by a momentary panic. There wasn't an alarm, you just woke up naturally. Wondering what day it even is.

Reach over and grab your phone, it's quarter to ten already, Wednesday. Your day off. The panic subsides and you close your eyes, basking in the possibilities of the unplanned stretch of day sitting before you.

You still feel the hangover of a heavy shift the night before. The sharp ache in the bottom of your feet is a reminder of the back and forth, back and forth. Your hands are cracked and sore from repeatedly plunging glasses in and out of shelves and dishwashers.

The disappointing sandwich, hastily stuffed down after midnight, leaves a nauseous trace in your stomach. But you can't let that hold you back, it's your day off. Open your eyes again, don't let the seconds turn to minutes while you lie in bed, even though you'd like nothing more.

Days off are stressful. You're supposed to be working it all out. The job is just tiding you over and bringing some cash in while you figure out the bigger picture. Your day off is when you make plans, get things done and carve out what comes next.

This is the time to work out exactly what is at the bottom of that cliff and how you stop yourself from drowning. The problem is, you just want to close your eyes and go back to sleep, maybe have some lunch, and watch TV.

The mental battle lasts a few minutes before you eventually will yourself to get up and throw some clothes on. The shredded skin on the back of your heels throbs as you hobble down the stairs.

The house is peaceful, everybody's at work. At least you've got some space to do your own thing before they come home with the inevitable barrage of questions.

Find any jobs? Do you need help with your CV? Are you qualified for that? Do people even pay you for that?

Don't worry about that now. First order of the day is coffee and breakfast. Munch slowly through a bowl of cornflakes, savouring each bite, putting off your responsibilities with every deliberate crunch.

You only get halfway through the bowl before it turns into an anaemic mush that goes straight in the bin. Sip at your coffee and gaze out of the window while you think of more delay tactics. Can't do anything until you've had a shower, you'll feel fresher and more focused.

Normally, you're a quick five minutes in and out, but this morning, you spend twenty minutes in there.

Eyes closed, the sound of the rushing water blocks everything else out for a while. Standing inside the wall of white noise, you still feel that expectation tapping you on the shoulder. The day is fast slipping away.

By the time you get out and get dressed, it's already eleven o'clock. Not long until lunch, but now, it's time to be productive, after making another coffee to help you focus.

Sit down at your desk and open your laptop. Lost fingers hover over the keyboard. The cursor in the search bar flashes, waiting for you to decide. A whole world of possibilities and you haven't got a clue where to start. Everybody else has pitched in with their ideas, you didn't like the sound of them but it's a place to start at least.

What was it dad suggested? You shake your head slightly as you type 'speedboat repair 'into Google. After a few minutes of skim reading articles and coming up against endless qualifications and training hurdles, you realise that you never liked that idea anyway.

What about Uni again? That's the ticket to something according to everybody. Another quick search and you're faced with a daunting list of degrees that sound just as dull as the one you already dropped out of. You don't want to be sat in a classroom anyway, doing the same thing day in, day out. You want excitement, no two days the same. Getting out there and getting your hands dirty doing... something.

Apprenticeships, that's the new thing. Learn on the job, get stuck in. You scroll through the list of available courses and yet again, you're met with hundreds of possibilities, all of them devoid of any creativity.

It's exhausting doing mental gymnastics, trying to convince yourself that you're interested in anything you find. You latch onto any tiny positive and start creating stories in your head, elaborating on the shred of interest and justifying all the things you know you'd hate about the job.

What you need right now is money and something that you don't dread waking up for, you can sort the rest out later. Take things one step at a time, get a slightly better job that isn't as tiring and you'll find it easier to work out your passion.

Open your old CV, untouched since you were sixteen. It's a sparse white wasteland of empty jargon and minor accomplishments stretched out into bloated paragraphs.

You look through and try to think of things to add. Blast out a few lines about working as a waiter. Add some bullshit about organisational skills and customer service. It hardly makes a dent on the empty space. What else can you add?

Dropped out of Uni? Excellent at wasting time? Zero direction whatsoever.

Scroll to the bottom and look at the hobbies and interest's section. Hesitate for a moment before putting 'writing poetry. ' Delete it and close the page.

Look at the time. It feels like you've been at it all day but it's only been an hour. You should carry on, put the time in so you can avoid the hassle when everybody gets home from work.

You manage about ten minutes of sorting through lists of job titles that don't mean anything. There are a thousand different names for unfulfilling office job and none of them are as important as they sound.

The switch from job sites to social media is seamless, you almost don't notice it happening. The action is the same. Look at a post, acknowledge it with barely a reaction. Move onto the next. Repeat.

For a while, you get lost in the manufactured adventures of others, living through them, trying to convince yourself that it's enough. But it doesn't last long. Soon, it just becomes another reminder that you're stuck and you need to drag yourself out of this rut.

Once you've already given up on the job search and started procrastinating online, it's easy to give up on the pretence altogether. You start rummaging around your room, looking through old drawers and reliving childhood memories.

Tell yourself the obvious lie that you're looking for inspiration. Going back to your childhood and trying to recapture the things that sparked your imagination back then. Maybe if you could remember what you used to want, before everybody started telling you what you should want, things would be clearer.

But in the end, you waste the next few hours flicking through an old Beano comic and watching the first half of Pulp Fiction. For the first time, it starts to feel like a day off, but the guilt ruins it.

Time is ticking away and you're still no closer to a solution that will satisfy them. You've got another shift tomorrow and there won't be time to get anything done in the morning. That time is dead space, reserved for mentally preparing yourself.

It's so easy to slip into the trap, letting the days turn into weeks, the weeks turn into months. Slowly but surely, you stop trying and people stop pushing. The stop gap becomes the destination.

You need to get out for a bit, clear your head and then come back to it with more energy. You've still got a few hours until everybody gets back and when they do, you'll have something to show for it.

It's a nice day, not too hot but there's no need for a jumper. You wander aimlessly for a while, dip into the shop for a drink and then find a bench.

As you watch everybody going about their day, headed to and from work, you envy them. Their lives seem so simple- they get up, go to work, head home to their family.

But you're not unique in this. Every person that you watch go by has, at some point, found themselves lost, trying to decide on a path without really knowing what's at the end of it. A lot of them made the wrong choice and stuck with it, but at least you didn't do that.

Failure is a funny thing, and most people don't understand it. Where you are right now is, in the eyes of most people, a failure. But that isn't true, it's a beginning. Sure, you don't know what it's the beginning of, but you decided to live a happy and fulfilled life doing something that you wanted to do.

You sit for a while, sorting through ideas in your head and trying to decide what you want your life to be.

In the end, it's simple. You want things to be interesting, you want to feel like you're leaving some kind of mark on the world, no matter how small. Having the next ten years of your life mapped out in detail isn't important, you just want to know that you're stable enough to grab any opportunity that presents itself.

Still, this doesn't really help with the here and now, the practical question of what you're going to do.

As you sit there, mulling it over and watching people drift by, you feel a shot of inspiration hit you. Take out your phone and start jotting down notes. Words and phrases are crafted into flowing sentences. Bits are deleted and reworked, shuffled around or thrown out entirely until you are left with the bare bones of something new.

Smile to yourself and put the phone away, noticing the time as you do. You've only got an hour and a half until they get back and you haven't really made any progress, at least, that's what you think.

You neck the dregs of a lukewarm bottle of coke and chuck it in the bin on your way past as you head for home. Get in, make another coffee to help you concentrate, open your laptop and pick up where you left off. Dip in and out of job sites, giving things a cursory glance.

Even though you can't put your finger on it, you have a sense of what you're looking for. Something creative, the kind of thing that people would describe as 'not a proper job, ' whatever that means. You're desperately hoping to find gold in amongst the dirt, but you won't.

You figure that you should at least apply for something, just so you have a record of the day- proof that you're taking your future seriously and trying to find some direction.

You open a few different tabs, the kinds of jobs you think they'll approve of, and start filling out the basic information on the forms. You make it to the second page where they start asking the tough questions like 'why do you want to work here? 'before you give up. Tell yourself you've made a start and that's progress.

Back to the CV, read it over and over. Delete bits and then reword them without adding anything new. Change the font a few times and add some headings. Google CV tips and leave the tab open as more evidence.

The whole time you're creating this facade, you can feel it nagging you in your pocket. Your phone, holding the seed of a new idea ready to be watered. No more procrastination, you tell yourself. Nobody's paying you for that, you'd be the richest man in the world if they did.

Need to knuckle down and stop distracting yourself from what's important. It'll take you a little while longer to realise that you got things upside down.

Eventually, you give in and shut the laptop. You spend the rest of the afternoon laid on your bed, rewriting and honing it until you're satisfied. For the first time all day, you feel a spark of excitement about something.

None of the hundreds of job listings you glanced at gave you the same buzz. Capturing the world and your place in it in a few short lines feels worthwhile. Whether you show it to anybody or not, you've created something. It exists and it will always exist, even after you're gone, and the phone is buried under tons of rubbish in a landfill somewhere. You brought forth an idea into the world in an afternoon, how many people can say the same?

Once you're finished, you set the phone down and decide to watch the rest of Pulp Fiction. You've seen it a hundred times before but that's what you want right now. The strained sleep pattern, long shifts, and the endless job hunt are taking their toll on you. You're not in the mood for something new or challenging, you just want the comfort of familiarity for a while.

It's not long before you drift off to sleep and you only wake when you hear the door go. Mum shouts your name and you jump up. Switch the TV off, open the laptop, shout back down and tell her you'll just be a minute.

She's in the kitchen making a cup of tea when you go down. She offers you one and you tell her to sit down, you'll make them. It's not long before the inevitable questions start coming.

"Did you find anything?"
"Yeah, a few things. Just filling out the applications."

You pass her the tea as you answer. She nods behind it and takes a sip. You weren't that convincing and when she starts probing you further, you struggle to remember what it was you were looking at. All the boring jobs merge together and you blurt out a string of garbled buzzwords. It sounds surprisingly like the job descriptions you've been struggling to pay attention to all day.

She listens along and smiles, but you can tell that she's frustrated inside. You were talking for a few minutes but all she heard is 'I've done nothing all day. 'More well-meaning suggestions follow, and you tell her that you'll start on those tomorrow if you have time before work.

The door goes again and dad comes in. You prepare yourself for another barrage of questions and this time, you make it sound a bit more convincing.

Notice a look between them, mum's slight eyebrow raise says 'that means he's done nothing. '

He comes at you with another list of suggestions that miss the mark but, again, you tell him that you'll get straight on it.

Excuse yourself and tell them that you're going to keep looking for a while before tea.

Back in your room, you sit staring at the application forms, forcing yourself to put something down, even though you know that you won't get the job and you don't want it. You can hear them downstairs, talking about you in a low whisper, wondering what they're going to do.

After a few failed attempts at filling out applications, you open a new tab and stare at the blank search bar. You almost don't want to type it because then you'll eventually have to explain it. They'll ask where you're going, you'll tell them and then they'll realise you're serious about it. It'll be endless reasons why it's not a good use of your time. They'll do that thing where they think they're being realistic but really, they're just being negative.

But it doesn't matter. You know it's the only time you feel anything close to fire in your belly. Eventually, you think, fuck it. You type 'local poetry classes 'in and start scrolling through the results.

You get more lectures at the dinner table that night and they keep telling you that you need a plan. In the back of your mind, you have half a plan. Maybe plan isn't the right word. You don't say anything because it's too hard to explain and you don't think they'll understand it anyway. You're not giving them enough credit, though. They won't understand, it's alien to them, but they'll try.

You head to bed early, hoping to a get a good night's sleep before your shift tomorrow. You rewind the film and watch the bit you missed when you had your afternoon nap.

It finishes and the credits roll, but you're not tired. It's getting late and you know that you need to sleep, but instead, you take out your phone and carry on writing. You'll pay for it tomorrow when you're three hours into an eight-hour shift and you're already exhausted but right now, you're locked into your own world and nothing outside of it matters.

Mum and dad are lying in bed, wide awake, stressed that you're not getting anywhere. From their point of view, you've achieved nothing today. You're no closer to finding your dream career and writing a roadmap for the next fifty years of your life. You haven't even got the faintest idea of what jobs you want to apply for or whether you want to go back to uni. You're floating in the wind and it scares them, but most of all it frustrates them.

You lie there, reading the new poem over and over, making the final tweaks and enjoying the way that one-line flows into the next.

They think you've achieved nothing today, but that isn't true.

JOHN FROM CALIFORNIA

I smelled you before taking in the rag tag sight. Nicotine tar and lighter fluid perfume should have prepared the poetry room for your entry, a horrific sensory fanfare alerting the innocent to your approach.

John from California.

Late into our lesson but that doesn't lessen your cocky persona, wiping sweat from sticky skin you snatch my hand and proclaim "what's the happy happs", I stagger my reply for the breath burning my eyes and the bile in my throat, seriously talking like a child at 45 wins you no prize.

John from California.

5 minutes of speech and you have interrupted each good idea and interesting opinion with "oh, ah, well, uhhhm" crescendo-ing into arrogant half-baked wonderings that leave the class stagnant and in need of a jump-start.

John from California.

I have to speak up with 10 minutes left to get this pompous nicotine reek to sit quiet before the docile poetry class goes on a wordy riot. You are so full of self-reward you have ignored the critic help that could save you from our scorn, but nope, he keeps pace and insults

145

In your head, everything was different.

You pictured an old lecture theatre, it's dim walls covered with ornate wood panels. At the front, a young professor in a corduroy blazer leans on the desk, patiently dipping the arm of his glasses in his mouth. He welcomes you to the course with the lines of some long-forgotten poet, takes the class outside when it's sunny and encourages dancing under the moonlight as homework.

It's a huge sense of relief then when you walk through the door at the end of the hallway. A series of tables wind in a U shape around the class, with half a dozen people dotted around, chairs all facing into the middle. The room stops as they smile and welcome you to take a seat.

The room is dimly lit by a fluorescent strip and two small windows at the back. Outside the sky is dark and grey, but the atmosphere in the room is relaxed, like you were all friends at a coffee shop or something. You pull up a chair two along from a woman in her thirties and wrestle out of your coat.

It's hard to make out who the teacher is but your bet is the older guy with his Barbour coat sitting along from you, the one leaning on a cane and staring into space. Any second now you expect him to spring to life.

"Alright. I think this is everyone."

A rosy cheeked lady beside the old man stands up and draws the attention of the class. Her wavy brunette hair hangs over the table as she scans a list of names on a sheet of paper.

The old fella with the cane opens his eyes, a little surprised at his own dosing off. He shakes his head and pulls a black notebook and pen from his coat.

"Well, we're one short. But I think we can just get started."

She looks around the room with a smile that settles the sudden panic burning in your ears. She can't be much older than you, maybe five years or so, but holds the floor in a way you never could.

"Now, I'm noticing a couple new faces today. So why don't we go around and briefly introduce ourselves."

There is a murmur of agreement around the table. She smiles and closes the binder with the register in it.

"So, hello everyone, my name is Victoria and I've been a writer ever since I was a young girl. I've had three collections published so far and I've been teaching here coming up to 3 years now."

The room knowingly nod their heads. Victoria turns to the old man beside her. Leaning on his cane, he shuffles forward and clears his throat.

"Right, I'm Allan. I've been writing since, oh... Since I retired, I think."

He nods and settles back into his chair. Victoria smiles at the lady sitting beside you.

"I'm June. I've got two daughters, Kayleigh and Sarah. I've only been writing for about a year, but I love it."

Victoria thanks her for the contribution. All eyes in the room settle on you. Your voice tightens as you introduce yourself and smile. A valve opens in your chest and all the concern you carried in with you rushes out.

"I don't know how long I've really been writing poems for. Sometimes I'm not even sure what I have are poems. I guess that's why I'm here."

You feel the words balloon from your mouth and float in the air. Looking around the room, you see that same worry on every single face, even Victoria's.

The last of the group introduce themselves. You sit there, red-faced and staring at the wall a thousand yards away.

Victoria moves to stand behind her chair. She pauses for a moment then approaches the board at the front. In block capitals she scrawls four letters across the empty white space. P O E M.

"I think something valid came up there. How do you know when you've written a poem?"

She clicks the lid back on and lets the question hang there. She twirls the pen between her fingers and looks around the room.

"When I was in Uni, we had this lecturer. Kath something. One day a person in my class asked how to write poems properly."

She turns and begins to pace the narrow space between the tables. Stopping to lean on a desk, she folds her arms and looks at the ceiling.

"She said just write until it looks like one. It might not seem like it but that's kind of all there is to it."

She laughs and unfolds her arms, moving back behind the desk and leafing through a small bundle of papers.

"I think the important thing to take away from this is that there are no..."

A knock at the door. A black cloud darkens the sky and hurls heavy drops of rain against the window. The door creeps open. Before you even see him, the pungent air sweeps in and claims the room.

"Hey there."

His greeting cuts through the silent space. You hear the sands of Californian beaches and pull of the riptide dripping in his voice, an unreal parody of America booming across the class.

"Sorry I couldn't find parking."

Victoria nods and motions him into the room.
He saunters in, taking the long route around the tables, eventually dropping in the seat right beside you.
Up close, you can see the deep tan wrinkles pulling at the skin around his eyes. The stench of stale fags morphs into something unbearable as he takes off his coat, the damp air around him like a living, breathing skin.
He smiles at you. You return the greeting, but you can't stop it turning into a grimace.
Victoria stands behind the desk, unsure of the point she was trying to make. She drums her nails on the surface and smiles.

"Well, let's not waste any time and get right to it."

She walks back into the centre of the room, everyone's eyes following her path between the tables. She stops somewhere in the middle and casually scans each face.

"Last week we were looking at poems about cities. Does anyone want to share what they were working on?"

After a pause, June raises her hand. She takes out a small wad of paper and hands it across to Victoria, who walks around the room laying the sheets in front of everyone. By the time she reaches you, there is only one left.

"Would you gents mind sharing?"

The paper glides across the table. His murky hand catches it and thrusts the sheet between you. He leans across and grabs your hand.

"What's the Happy-happs. I'm John."

His limp hands are damp with sweat, pawing at your fingers. You're surprised your hand doesn't slide right out of his grip. There's no chance to say your name before he's turned back to the poem lying there between you. His damp leg brushes up against you.

"Let's read this poem then buddy."

He's like a stray cat, damp from the rain and rubbing his scent everywhere. Hold your breath and try to read from a safe distance.

Victoria pulls out her seat and gently places herself behind the table, her attention falling on the poem.

"Just take five minutes with it. What do you like about it? What could be made better?"

The room is still, almost silent except from your heavy mouth breathing. You thought it might help, but it's no good. He has managed a scent so strong you can taste it, there in the back of your mouth- like you lifted a cig butt from a puddle and ate it.

Turn to the poem, its title 'Scarborough Fair' stamped in thick letters across the top of the page. You must read the first line about five times before you take anything in.

John runs his finger over the sheet, stacks of beads, bracelets and festival bands rattling as he goes. Falling back to the chair, he plants his hands on his head and stares at the ceiling, pretending to have an original thought.

You take the opportunity to ignore him and concentrate on the poem instead. After reading the first stanza twice, you feel his eyes burning into the back of your head.

He coughs to clear his throat, the thick phlegm slaps into his mouth and he swishes it around. Your eyes are shut, desperately imagining yourself someplace far away from him.

"Alright, now in groups of two, I just want you to take a minute to talk your thoughts through before we come together. OK?"

Force your eyes towards the caricature next to you, a phony smile plastered across his leather face. Despite smelling like forty a day, his teeth are pristine white. He scootches his chair at an angle.

"So guy, what did you think?"

It's hard to think of something to say. Every muscle in your body wants to move, pick up your bag and clamber to the other side of the room. But you don't. Instead, you pretend to think for a moment, letting your eyes blankly take in the page on the table.

"Yeah, I thought it was..."
"Didn't you just love how she makes you feel the place?"
"Yeah, I guess."

He leans over the table and runs his finger down the stanzas. His fingernails are chewed down to the bone, but still manage to trap dirt underneath.

"It's totally in your face, you know?"

You nod your head like you've taken on his point, but really all you can think about is what he means by in your face? You didn't think anyone talked like that anymore. But here he is, in the living, stinking flesh.

"I dunno, I thought it was quite sarcastic at points. Like she didn't..."
"What do you mean by sarcastic?"

Does he want a definition? He hunches over his knees, resting a fist under his chin. You lean back in your chair, speaking while trying not to breathe in.

"You know, like it was taking the piss a little bit."

An odd silence falls in the space between you. John nods his head for a contemplative moment, staring at the poem. You shift your eyes around the room at the three other groups, buried in friendly discussions about the work.

"Maybe I just don't get it."

He smiles through piercing white teeth and starts to laugh.

"Back in California, we're too happy for sarcasm."

He howls like an overexcited child, slapping the table as he laughs. You feel everybody glance at the wild American in the room and feel guilty by association. He simmers down and shuts his eyes to bask in the moment.
You try reign him in with a meagre laugh.

"So what did you think?"

Both eyes pierce open with dramatic flair. You regret the words instantly- this could go on for hours. He scans over the page again, mouthing the words under his breath. Leaning back, his eyes drift towards the ceiling.

"What do I think... What do I think... Well..."

You're unsure whether he's stalling or the question has genuinely confused him. He crosses his arms and clicks his tongue, unable to cultivate thought without a fanfare of noises and drama.

"See, I think what you're saying is interesting, but I'm not sure it's right."

It knocks you back a little. Here you were expecting to receive some long, self-important ramble; not to be told your idea was wrong. Flat out, no ifs or buts, just in your face feedback - wrong.

A quiet sigh sinks the weight on your shoulders. You consciously force your jaw to unclench and fingers to loosen around the pen.

Having gathered himself, allowing for the necessary dramatic pause, he goes on.

"I honestly think, and this is just my opinion, but I think she loves the place she's writing about. It's so vibrant and alive. Like can you not just feel that oozing from the page?"

A stray hand strokes the poem, his fingers tracing each line. The whole time, he keeps his eyes trained on your face, his heavy stare willing you to agree with him. Your knee starts to shudder as you rest your head in your hand on the table.

"Yeah, I guess."

As the room winds up their conversations, Allan cracks a joke which sets him and June off laughing, his cane rapping on the floor with each chuckle. Victoria takes this as a cue to move to the floor again.

"Right, so I hope we've all had a chance to talk through our thoughts. Would anyone like to start us off?"

Silence.

Suddenly, you feel like you're in school again, stuck next to a person you can't stand and racking your brain for something worth saying. There's a comfort in that brittle silence though, a sense of solidarity in the fact that no one wants to go first, even John.

Victoria looks around the room. She knows the silence only too well and turns to June.

"Ok, how about you introduce the piece for us and we can go from there."

Everyone shifts their attention to her. Suddenly, the confident Yorkshire voice becomes softer, talking at the table.

"Well, I'm originally from Scarborough. When we talked about writing about a city, it was the only place I could think of to write about. I know it's not a city or that, but it's home, I guess."

John clears his throat, interrupting her with a long drawn out -

"Ah. Well... I really got the sense that you love the place."

June scans over the poem like she's missing something. The other groups pass a look to each other, then the poem and finally John. You keep your focus fixed on the board, eyes tracing the four letters hanging there.

"Scarborough? I mean, it's home but it's a bit shit. When I tried to write about it, I just ended up taking the piss."

Victoria leans on the table across from June, arms crossed and nodding her head. She pulls the page from the table and holds it like a declaration.

"I think it's an interesting way to write about a place. Often as readers we are an outsider looking in. Humour can be very good at taking the unfamiliar and making it tangible to the reader."

155

June lowers her eyes, fighting back a nervous smile. In the quiet moment, she studies her own poem, seeing it in a new light. Something like pride straightens her shoulders and sits her up straight.

From beside you there is a stuttering-

"Ah, uh. Well, the way I read it was that, you know, you were seeing like, all the beauty in the everyday of Scar-Bur-Ough."

John punches the name into three overly American syllables. Bury your face into your hands, fingertips soothing the ache building quietly behind your eyes.

"But maybe I'm still not used to the irony you Brits are so famous for."

Keep your eyes shut like this, digging your fingers into the quiet darkness of your vision and letting the swirls of grey pressure block you from his voice.

"Like you just wouldn't get a poem like this back home. The folk are too earnest to, what do you guys say, 'take the piss?'"

He punctuates the last part with air quote fingers. Suddenly every group breaks off into their own private whisperings and ideas on the poem. Allan leans towards June and mentions how he hasn't been to Scarborough since the seventies.

Your eyes open and fix on the clock. The lesson ticks past the half-way point, and your American neighbour has managed to single-handedly derail any and every point so far.

Victoria pulls the conversations to a close and takes her place in front of the board. The marker twirls between her fingers as she paces from one side of the board to the other.

"Now I think we should stick to the theme of poems about where we all come from."

On the board she rings a circle around the word Poem and branches a line into a free space. For the first time all lesson, you start to write something in your fresh notebook.

"So, these are maybe some questions we can ask ourselves as we start with our pieces. What do our readers know about the place? What do only we know about it? What senses are we experiencing in your work? Like June, can we maybe use humour to explore the more personal sides of our worlds?"

The lid clicks back on the pen, she stops to survey the board and turns with a welcoming smile on her face.

"Can anyone think of anything else?"

A familiar silence falls across the class. John starts to scratch his chin, a parody of a man with thoughts.

"Well, I was thinking that..."

Your own interjection startles you. Pause for a moment, deliberating on the exact way to phrase your thoughts.

"Like could you use a different point of view?"

John scoffs quietly enough that only you hear it and leans back on his chair with his arms crossed. You think about just how easy it would be to tip him back, letting him fall into the void of his own self-satisfaction.

Victoria nods her head, her smile beaming to the back of the dim room. It's hard not to find her positive attitude infectious as she clicks the lid off again.

"I think that's a good idea. Any point of view in particular?"

A hundred ideas flood in, the million different viewpoints of a place pin-balling inside your head. For once, you begin to feel excited by uncertainty, the infinite possibilities before you and none of them right or wrong.
The chair legs snap to the floor beside you.

"Ah, oh erm. I was thinking that..."

As he unleashes his rambling again, your excitement fades. The plethora of ideas die, one by one until only one remains. Your eyes fall on the page with a single line scrawled across the first line.

How to write a poem...

You close the notebook and lay down the pen. Eyes closed, you picture yourself shutting the mouth of John from California, forever.

SKIN DEEP CONFIDENCE

You've never met a room you can't control or a crowd you couldn't hold in the palm of your hand because you understand the power of a story. You can make them see glory, feel joy, sadness or be inspired. You're social to the soul, gregariously wired.

But I can see, at a glance, your confidence is skin deep. Your vulnerability seeps, through the cracks in your make up. That's why you always need to shake up the group. In case they find these stories you've refined aren't just popping into your mind, but primed and ready to go on demand. You wear your stories like armour so no one will find out that beneath your skin-deep confidence is a foundation of self-doubt.

In a few hours, the landlord in the King's Arms will be on his feet, darting through crowds of punters to restock drinks as fast as they can drink them.

The younger guy behind the bar will move zombie minded as the night wears on, pouring a drink with one hand while punching money in the till with the other.

Notes will fly, drinks downed and empties stacking up high on the bar. But for now, the pub with a half-dozen regulars staring at their lone pint glasses has a still quality.

The landlord sits on a stool at the end of the bar, his face buried in his phone. He's nursing a coke, but in a bit the first pint will come. You've been coming here long enough to know that the man drinks like clockwork.

Coming in from the beer garden, you loop around the stray stools and head for the bar. Faces of the sad old punters rise from their pints and watch you navigate the tables and rest your arms on the brass. One of them shakes his head and nurses a slow sip of ale.

The lad behind the bar puts down his phone and rests an arm on the Stella tap. You lift the rim of your hat and scan over the taps like you need a minute to think.

"Erm. Three Guinness and a rum and coke."

You reach into the stiff pocket of your white jeans for your wallet.

"Oh, and a gin and tonic please."

He nods and starts to work on it. At the end of the bar, the landlord lays down his phone and downs the rest of his coke. He calls out to the barman.

"Do us a Guinness as well pal."

For a quiet moment, he looks you up and down.

"Bit early for Halloween, isn't it?"

Laugh and take the hat off your head.

"Off to a fancy-dress party after."

You pass the bowler hat across and he tries it on.
He shouts behind the bar.

"What d'you reckon?"

The lad looks up from the pint.

"Jesus Christ man"

He stops the tap and stares at him.

"You look like a posh twat."

He tosses the hat on the bar and the three of you laugh. The phone on the side vibrates and his eyes are dragged back to the screen.

You pay up and load the drinks onto a sticky black tray. He reaches across with your change.

"It's a class film that though."

He nods to the bowler hat on the bar.

"Not got a cane?"
"Left it outside."

You put the hat on and lift the tray.

"Cheers fellas."

Turn and make for the beer garden. Froth from the pints slides down the edge of the glass. The oversized wine glass sloshes the gin from side to side and the coke fizzes as you navigate your way back through.

A wave of smoke hits you as you push through the door and step outside. High above your head, a vent churns hot damp air over the small concrete beer garden. On the picnic table below, your pals' laughter echoes off the wall and fills the dead space.

"There he is."

You lay the tray on the table, clap your hands and rub them together.

"Right, so that's a Guinness for Shaggy and Velma. A gin for Mr Snow and the rum for Action Man."

"Fuck off, it's Rambo."

"Sure thing Soldier." Velma butts in.

Rambo shakes his head and lights another cig. You slide into the bench and lift your glass.

"Cheers guys."

Their drinks meet you in the middle.

Jon takes a massive swig from the gin. He starts to fumble with the cloak and fur around his neck, cheeks bulging as he sighs into the sky.

"Fucking boiling in this thing."

Shaggy searches in his pockets and lays a pouch of tobacco on the table. Velma grabs it and starts to roll a cigarette. She looks at Jon as she fiddles with a strip of filters.

"What did you say you were again?"

"Can you not guess?"

Jon spreads his arms under the cloak.

"I've no idea."

She stuffs strands of tobacco in the skin and rolls it between her fingers.

"Is this some Lord of the Rings thing?"

"Eh, close enough."

Shaggy takes the pouch off Velma and starts to roll his own.

"Are you mental?" Jon looks genuinely offended. "Easy now."

You grab the cane from beside you and make a large gesture with it.

"A tantrum is coming."
"Fuck off."

He fights a smile into his gin, takes a swig and lets the cubes rattle together.

You've known Rambo and Jon Snow since school, Shaggy you met later in college. You weren't really friends at first, just a face you'd pass in the hall. It wasn't until you became regulars at this place that you really got to know each other.

The four of you used to haunt this bench, fingers clutching cheap pints at every opportunity. Other faces would come and go, but in that brief window before Uni you were fixtures here.

Then you and Shaggy got accepted and those long nights chatting shit became a funny story filed in your head under My Mates Back Home. You remember that feeling when you were away, talking to strangers about your life before like it was some distant memory.

Since you've been back, you've hardly caught sight of Jon and Rambo as their quiet office life slowly shrinks their free time to Friday nights. On the odd occasion you go for a pint, you still see flashes of the past cutting through the mundane routines.

You've never met Velma before.

Course you'd seen the odd post online, a picture of them with their arms wrapped over each other as you sat in bed alone, mindlessly scrolling.

Another Uni relationship, the story of Halls, nights out and names you don't know in a two-person bundle. Seeing them here together, you can see the future.

They'll graduate and move in together. You'll see less of them and when you do, they'll be talking about mortgages and dogs. The awkward silences will grow longer as you realise that your lives are slowly drifting apart.

Then one day you'll be invited to stumble through conversations at their wedding and answer awkward questions - just like tonight.

"So, are you at Uni as well?"

Shaggy and Velma stare at you through a drag on their cigs. The others busy their eyes as if you might get embarrassed by the question.

It figures, you'd not really spoken to Shaggy in a while, let alone the other two. It was a surprise to hear he was coming tonight. It was already happening. A waft of smoke catches the back of your throat. You hold in the cough and settle it with a swig.

"I was in Uni, yeah."

You've not had to say those words for a while now. You know how the rest of the conversation will go, with your half rehearsed a hundred times or more.

"But it wasn't for me."
"Just not fancy it?"
"Something like that."

You roll the base of your glass on the table.

"I had fun and everything but…"

There's only so long you can take the isolation.
Shake the thought away.

"Guess the course wasn't for me."

The table nod their heads as Velma takes another swig of her pint. Rambo starts to count his cigs while debating another. Shaggy studies you over a long, thoughtful drag.

"So, what are you doing now?"

Rambo and Jon look at each other and laugh. It's infectious, spreading to Velma and even cracking your face a little.

"I'm waiting tables for now."

A huge grin spreads across Shaggy's face.

"Who gave you that job?"

 The others catch on to his excitement and laugh.

"Clumsiest man I know and they let you carry stuff for money?"

Their cheers echo off the high concrete wall and into the fading red sky. You act shocked, but the reaction is the same every time.

"Now in fairness…"

Jon swoops his cloak to the side and points at the door.

"Did you see the way he carried the drinks in there? Proper professional."
"I dunno…"

Shaggy lifts his pint and inspects it.

"I've seen better heads on a Guinness."
"Well, I didn't pour the thing."

You sit up straight, staring at the head on your own pint.
It's a bit big.

"I'm a dab hand on the taps, actually."

You tip the rim of your bowler hat.

"Gonna need to see this."

Shaggy docks his cig and takes a moment with his drink.
You all do, a quiet minute between old faces, all enjoying
the familiarity of this beer garden, the chat, and the promise
that tonight could be a laugh. Rambo picks at his nail, his knee
is rattling under the table. He desperately needs tonight to be
a laugh. Velma looks at Shaggy and breaks the silence.

"You had a trial as a waiter."

She breaks into a knowing smile and turns to the rest of
you.

"Has he told you about this?"
"Think I managed half an hour before they asked me to
leave."

Shaggy lets out a small chuckle and takes a slow draw of
beer.

"Guess I must be a natural."

You say, trying to act casual. Don't let on that the long
nights on your feet are slowly draining you.

166

"There was this guy the other night though, absolutely reeked of piss."

Velma coughs her Guinness back in the glass. Rambo looks over the rim with a scrunched face and sees off the drink.
Swirl the head clinging to the sides of the glass and clear your throat. They're hooked.

"So, the whole night, no one wants to serve this guy. They all figure it's him, so they stick him right at the back of the place. And guess who's lumped with serving him?"

Jab a thumb in your chest and smile. Rambo shakes his head.

"Nah, couldn't do it. I'd be showing him the door."
"This is it though right."

Push your pint to the side and start moving your arms to the rhythm of the story, acting out each line.

"This man is a heavy drinker. So, every time I go over, I have to stop just out of sight and..."

Take a deep breath and hold it. Bulge out your cheeks and speak in a nasal-high voice to the imaginary man.

"What can I get you?"

Nod your head as he gives his order. Let the breath escape you.

"Same thing every time; Pint of John Smiths and a Brandy."

Velma nudges along the bench, wrapping Shaggy's arm around her waist. Rambo decides against the half-cig in hand and offers it to Jon, he refuses and turns back to you.

"So, it's getting on a bit, he must be about five or six deep and my manager cuts him off. Course he doesn't say that, so I have to go up and tell him."

You are in the flow of it now, the memory of this guy alive at the table with you.

"So, I walk up to the table and give him the bill. But just before I can take the empties away, he grabs my arm and says thanks."

You let the last sentence hang in the air.

"Turns out his wife had just passed away. Poor guy had no fucking clue what to do with himself anymore. Like he's fighting back tears as he slips a twenty in my hand."

Your eyes drift down to the half Guinness on the table.

"I walk back over to the bar, get the man a double Brandy and tell him it's on the house."
"Jesus."

Shaggy shakes his head and squeezes Velma's waist.
The garden falls silent, you can hear the rumble of eager drinkers building inside the pub.

"So as this guy's on his way out, he stops to chat to my boss..."

Lift your pint. It's the last blow, the grand finale to the tale.

"Says what a great server I am, he's had a good night. Shame about the funny smell at the back there."

There's a faint chuckle that settles around the group, cutting through the sadness of it all.

"Never figured out what the smell was, but I reckon it wasn't him."
"Mate, dunno how you do it."

Rambo crushes the cig in the ashtray.

"Like serving the public. I couldn't deal with them."
"Eh, it's only bad some of the time."

Take a swig of Guinness to soothe the raspy throat you've earned.

"Pretty boring the rest of it."

Jon pulls his phone from inside the cape and reads a message.

"Right."

He slaps his hand on the table.

"Should we head out?"

The table uses this as an excuse to sup the last of their drinks. The Guinness lays heavy in your empty stomach, churning as you lean back to down the rest of the pint. Your empty glass cracks back to the wood and a sharp burp burns down the back of your throat.
Velma lifts her pint high and downs the rest in one go. She looks at shaggy.

"Just gimme a minute."

She slides out of the bench, adjusting the oversized orange jumper and pushing the empty black frames up her nose. As the door closes behind her, the sound of a full pub spills out into the garden.

"Gonna need to stop by a shop."

Rambo rattles the pack of cigs.

"And what's the deal with drinks tonight?"
"Should we get some beers in?"

Shaggy is speaking with his eyes fixed on the door Velma walked out of. It's hard to tell if he's more or less tense with her not around.

"Said they've made cocktails for the night."

You look across at Shaggy, but his attention left with Velma.

"Can't hurt to grab a few beers though."

Shaggy pulls himself back into the group.

"We getting a taxi up then?"
"Mate, it's down the road."

Jon laughs, it's only been half a year but he's acting as if he can't remember the place at all.
The door swings open, Velma walks out trailed by a Zombie with his arm wrapped around a Devil half his size.

"Well look who it is."

The Zombie calls out across the Garden. Velma and the Devil look uncomfortable, two complete strangers in a group of friends. The night is shaping up into a school reunion at this point.

Shaggy gets to his feet and throws his arms over the ripped clothes hanging loose on the Zombies body. He introduces Velma and wraps his arm around her. The Zombie names the Devil at his side.

Everyone's on their feet now, itching to get this part out the way and get the drinks going again.

"Alright then. Should we get moving?"
"Ah come on now. Only just got here."

The Zombie rubs his thick hands together.

"One for the road?"
"Shots?"

Velma gauges the reaction of the group.

"Right then"

Jon whips his hands from the cape and ushers everyone out the door.

"Shots then down the road we go."

It's packed inside now. Regulars line the bar and scrunch around tables, the week of work hanging heavy on their shoulders. They hardly look up from their pints as the mishmash of characters line up at the bar.

The Zombie leans against the brass and does a head count. He slides two twenties out of his wallet and holds them above the crowd. The landlord is still at the end, heavy set eyes scanning over the group. Zombie calls out to no one in particular.

"Seven Jaeger-bombs when you're ready pal"

The reaction of the group splits in two, some pre-gagging and the rest excited to get it down them.

The landlord rolls his eyes and plods behind the bar, lining up shot glasses.

"Aren't you lot a bit old for that these days?"

He leans into the fridge and cracks open the off-brand energy drink.

"This stuff is fucking poison, y'know?"

You lift the rim of your hat with the cane as a shot of Jaeger clinks into the glass.

Think of all the times you stood at this bar in the past, knocking back drinks with your mates without a care in the world. But looking around you, that atmosphere is gone.

The thick liquor in the glass doesn't look like the carefree possibility of youth anymore. It feels like a desperate fifty-year-old bloke wearing a pair of ridiculous trainers he saw in the video to a rap song he pretends to like.

The Zombie turns and dishes out shots to Velma and Shaggy, then yourself and the Devil, then finally Jon and Rambo. Shaggy stares at the glass, lifts it to his nose, gags and shakes his head. He holds the drink at an arm's length.

"Mate I can't do it. I'll be fucking sick if I try."

Under the white make-up and patchy flecks of fake blood, the Zombie looks offended, like he doesn't know the man anymore.

Reach out and take the drink from him.

"Cheers!"

Neck the first and try hold it down. The syrupy burn made worse by the warm sparkle of cheap energy drink mixing with Guinness in your gut.

The Zombie's face lights up. You join the group and down the second. Seven empty glasses slam onto the bar. Ignore the burn, the churning in your stomach- ignore the feeling and leave.

Outside, darkness settles over the streets. Taxis hurl past, rushing to fill the bars with as many bodies as possible. The group snakes its way along the road and stops at an offie.

Wait outside as they cram into the tight aisles of the shop to stock up on beer. More than drinks, you need the air to cool you and strip the feeling bubbling deep inside your stomach.

The energy you hide behind has fallen away with each step from the beer garden. The nostalgia is fast fading, replaced with a familiar numbness.

Rambo steps out of the door with a bottle of Vodka in one hand, a fresh pack of cigs in the other. He plants one in his mouth and lights up. He exhales into the cool night as a bus crashes past.

"I meant to say, there's jobs going at my place. If you fancy it, let me know. I can put a good word in."

"Thanks."

You nod, picturing yourself wrapped in a suit and tie, slouched body buried in a cubicle.

"I appreciate it."

He carries on, talking to himself mainly, gesturing with the end of his cigarette.

"It's not the most exciting, but the money's good. You've got to be realistic - you know?"

You keep nodding along, giving him the space to convince himself. What does realistic mean anyway? He cracks the vodka and forces a mouthful down.

"I'm hoping for a promotion soon. Just got to put the extra hours in, show them you're serious. You'd do well there."

There's a desperation in his voice, like he's begging you to say yes. He needs you to justify it for him.

"Yeah, like I said, I'll give it some thought."

Try to sound like you mean it, but your mind is made up.
He finishes a cigarette, takes a break to grimace through another mouthful of vodka, and then lights up another straight away. You stand in silence, waiting for the others to come.
Jon Snow spills out the door and kicks a stray Coke can through Rambo's legs. The two of them start a kickabout and Rambo comes back to life again.
Catch your reflection in the window of a parked car. The bags around your eyes are thick, with sharp black lines spreading from your right eye. Lean on the flimsy plastic cane and take a deep breath.
Picture the man in the car's reflection - suited up, tie on and desperation in his eye. He's acting like the Dolly Parton life is the one for him, lying to himself again.
Could you live that great lie - like you were happy? Or would you need to slip on a different persona, acting your way through every job like there was hope at the end of it? A hand slaps your back. Shaggy wraps his arm over your shoulder, the

other holding Velma tight. Rambo takes charge up the street and you follow.

THIS IS WHAT HAPPENS

This is what happens when unstoppable enthusiasm meets an immovable passion. When your impatience is constantly clashing with not wanting to rush because every moment needs appreciation and love but you're so sure the next moment will be better. You better believe it'll last forever because the thought of stopping feels the same as dying and I don't know what happens next. When nothing feels this good then next must never happen.

I've spent so long drifting through life on a boat with no captain, compass or maps. I thought perhaps I'd be lost forever, never knowing whether I was headed towards land or if the water just kept getting deeper and with no end in sight, my head went down, convinced I would drown. It was only when I looked up, I found I could navigate by starlight.

You burst through the door with more energy than usual. This isn't just another day checked-off on the calendar- it's bigger than that, a giant fucking boulder lifted off your chest.

The others give you a strange look as you bound towards the bar and greet them. They've never seen so much optimism at the start of an eight-hour shift.

Dial it back a bit, don't let on too early. Your boss comes through and gives you a brief nod before going to check the receipts from the night before. You don't need much direction- you know what you're doing.

You consider grabbing him now and just telling him. Drop the bomb early and then get on with your shift. It might make things awkward though and you don't want to end on a sour note.

It's not bad here, you've just got bigger plans. After tonight, you're going to hit the ground running and barrel headlong into a life of excitement and passion. Never quite knowing what tomorrow will bring and relishing in the fact.

Think back to your first shift- the anxiety you carried with that first tray, all eyes bearing down on you as you shuffled between tables. Then the exhaustion at the end of it, followed by a horrible sense that this might be it for you.

Every time you sat on the bus here felt like a sure sign you'd spend the rest of your life lost in a sea of mediocrity and missed chances.

But today is different. You might not have a clear bearing but you've got something more important - and you're ready for it to start.

All that's left to do is cut off the dead weight and steer yourself towards shore. Just wait until the end of your shift and tell him.

For now, there are tables that need setting up. You glide through the room with a spray bottle and a rag, wiping and straightening chairs as you go.

Dart across to the kitchen and start hauling trays of clean glasses into the bar. Everybody else trudges along, dragging out the hour of peace they get before the onslaught of impatient punters hits them. Until then your enthusiasm is grating.

Eventually, opening time comes and the early starters filter in. A couple of solemn old guys with spidery red cheeks head to the bar and order the usual. They've been killing time all morning, just waiting for midday to roll around.

They arrive at the same time every day, with the same newspaper, and the same pint. As you pull back on the pump and watch the jet of frothy brown ale splash into the bottom of the glass, you wonder whether they even remember what it feels like to take a risk.

Put the one down on the bar and he reaches for it before you even let go. His friend watches intently as you grab another glass and start pouring.

The repetitive motion of pulling the pump back is second nature to you now. It feels natural and, in a way, comfortable. It's easy to settle into the rhythm and watch the level of the beer creep up and over the rim.

They wait in silence, casually glossing over the headlines for their next conversation, the same as yesterday and the day before. And maybe they have it right.

Maybe a life of routine is what you need. Simple things, steady work and a pub to kill the rest of the time. Find a job you can tolerate and do it for fifty years. Who needs excitement when you can be secure?

But you're like a car with a dodgy engine, and the only one pushing it is you. Build up enough speed and you'll kick into gear, spluttering and coughing back to life. But as soon as you stop, the engine dies.

You put the second pint down and he hands over a tenner. He thanks you as you drop the coins into his hand. The other one coughs to clear his throat and points at the front page.

You rest against the bar for a moment and stare into the distance. The days are catching up with you and you're exhausted. You can't wait until you're old as these two to have your time be your own. You're young and need to start acting like it.

After a few minutes, you notice yourself drifting and shake yourself back into gear. Need to keep moving.

The back room is a mess, so you take the time to clean up before it starts getting busier and you're chained to the bar or running around tables for the rest of the afternoon. There are a few of your little champagne cork models sitting on top of a barrel in the corner. Put them in your pocket to keep as a souvenir.

You never did manage to finish your self-portrait. The malleable string of wire is still in the drawer at home somewhere, waiting to be worked and reworked again.

You manage to get the back room into good shape before your boss calls you through. The lunch orders are piling up and you head into the kitchen to start running plates.

Push through the clatter and heat to grab the food from under the hot glow of the lamps. Balance three plates as you wind between the tables and drop them off with the grace and professionalism of somebody that was born for this job.

Tables are starting to fill up and the noise of cutlery on ceramic rings through the room. For the next hour you don't stop. Fresh plates hit the table- dirty ones go back. More steaming food makes its way out. The till churns out bills, the card machine ticks over for a minute and spits out a receipt. Tear it off, have a nice day, scoop up the tip.

Round and round you go, bouncing from table to table, running like a well-oiled machine. Your manager watches from the bar, impressed with your newfound enthusiasm and a basic level of competence that you've never displayed before.

It hits 3 o'clock and the last few lunch orders start going out. You stride across the room with a steaming bowl of tomato soup sitting on the centre of your tray. You spot the old lady in the corner, waiting patiently with her spoon in hand. As you head towards her, you get lost in your head for a moment.

See, you're good at this when you put your mind to it. You never thought of yourself as a waiter really, just somebody that waits tables for a bit of cash until something better comes along. But today, you move through this job like you were born for it.

Maybe there is something noble here, maybe it's not just a stop gap. It could be a career. Work your way up to the top restaurants, get yourself a reputation as the best-

The thought comes crashing to a halt as your knee smacks into the back of a chair. The pain shoots all the way down your shin but you hobble on, trying to play it off as if nothing has happened. The tray jolts to the side and the bowl of soup threatens to go flying before settling back into place.

Look to your left and see two muscle-bound, bald-headed behemoths, locked into an intense conversation about football. One of them glances back at you as he feels the weight of your leg hit his chair.

"Sorry mate."

He frowns and goes back to his drink. His hooded jacket is draped over the back of his chair. You look at the bowl, now a little emptier than before. On second thoughts, this isn't the career for you.

Look back at the bar to see that, luckily, your manager is preoccupied with customers and hasn't noticed anything. Set the tray down on a nearby table and wipe the bowl with the corner of your apron. The old lady won't notice a bit missing.

She's happy to see her soup arrive and you head back into the kitchen, glad that you got away with it. The lunch rush is done with, and you've got a few hours until things pick up again.

Take the last few dirty plates into the kitchen and find the staff taking a well-earned breather before they need to prepare for the evening. Your manager pops his head around the corner and tells you to go on break while things are quiet.

Throw the apron on the side and head towards the door. A sandwich and a coffee will keep you going for the rest of your shift, you're halfway done now, just a few more hours until you can leave this place behind.

As you reach the front door, you hear a shout. You look back to see the man standing, with his hood up, tomato soup dripping down his face while his mate is doubled over, laughing. Dash out of the door before anybody can stop you.

The adrenaline rushes through your body as you push through the crowded streets. Nobody saw you, they won't know. Doesn't really matter now anyway. Stop in somewhere for a sandwich and a coffee and find a bench overlooking a small patch of grass.

Spend your hour watching the world go by, picking up on every small detail. The pigeons trot around, their heads darting back and forth as people rush by, dropping crumbs from rushed lunches. You smile at two of them, fighting over half a cold chip.

A woman wonders down the street with a handful of flyers, desperately trying to lock eyes with passers-by. She thrusts her hand towards people, and they veer around her as if she's contagious. She lets out a sigh, then spots you on the bench. There's nowhere to hide as she approaches you and shoves a flyer under your nose.

"Acting classes?"

You take it and smile. She turns back and continues trying to grab people on the street. You look at the flyer and flash back to that night, standing on stage, reading your poetry.

You thought you'd hate it before you got up there but once you were over that initial hurdle, there was something liberating about speaking to a group of complete strangers.

Fold the flyer into a small square and stash it in your back pocket. A smile creeps over your face as you continue watching people rush by.

Groups of friends march towards pubs, spurred on by the excitement of a long night ahead. Exhausted mothers drag kids from shop to shop, trying to tick everything off their list so they can head home and relax for five minutes. Tired workers slope towards the bus stop, desperate to get home and find some quiet.

In that moment, you feel content. This little snapshot of life is perfect, even if it isn't extraordinary. But soon the underlying anxiety comes back, poking you in the back of the head.

By now, your manager must have asked the rest of the staff, and somebody will remember you carrying that bowl of soup, even if they didn't see you spill it. They'll all be waiting for you to get back.

You wish you'd never started the job in the first place, it's not for you. For a few minutes, you sit there letting the scenario play out in your head over and over. What are they going to say when you get back?

It seems like the worst thing in the world right now but one day soon, it won't matter and you'll laugh about the poor soup-stained man and all the other stupid mistakes you made while you were trying to convince yourself that this job might be for you.

Still, the pangs of anxiety linger over you, but the excitement about today is still in there somewhere. You need to focus on that feeling, however small it is. Don't let anything get in the way and slow you down because slowing down feels like dying.

Be confident that you're making the right choice because you are, even though launching yourself into the unknown with no real sense of where you're going feels terrifying.

You don't want to get up, but your lunch hour is coming to an end. Just one last push and then you're out the door.

The atmosphere is different when you get back. Your manager glares at you as you come in, and no one is subtle about their whispered exchanges.

The walk from the door to the bar feels like it lasts forever. Nobody can prove it was you, but everybody knows.

Luckily, the victim has gone, probably placated with free drinks and grovelling. You give your manager a subdued nod as you grab the apron and head behind the bar. He says nothing.

A group of middle-aged women approach the bar and you busy yourself with a round of gin and tonics, keeping your head down and avoiding eye contact with the rest of the staff.

The women break ranks and stop cackling for a moment to pay for the drinks. Half of them disappear in one long slurp before they even get back to the table. You desperately look around and, for the first time ever, hope that more customers come in. But the place is empty, you're in that lull between lunch and the evening revellers, there's nobody to save you now.

Eventually, you're forced to turn around and look your manager in the eye as he walks towards you. Every step rattles the ground as he approaches and opens his mouth. Stand there like a naughty schoolboy with your hands in your pockets, twisting your trousers and staring into the ground.

Just let it roll over you. In one ear and out of the other, it doesn't matter in the grand scheme of things anyway. Except, it never comes.

He just tells you to do some clearing up in the back or something until it gets busier. Maybe you got away with it, but you can tell from his tone that he knows it was you and he's not going to forget about it. He's not angry, he's just disappointed.

Head into the back and pick up your normal routine of clearing away boxes and sweeping dust into the corner, ready to be blown about and swept up by the next person with half an hour to kill.

Drag the meagre amount of work out for as long as you can before deciding to have a sit-down for a bit. As you perch on the edge of an empty barrel, you feel something dig into your leg. You pull a crushed champagne cork figure from your pocket.

He looks a little sad and deflated. You lift him close to your face and study the twists and turns of his body. When you first made him, he was standing tall but now he's compressed, and he doesn't have the same confidence that he had before. He's running out of steam.

As you trace a finger along the twisted wire, you find yourself running out of steam too. The doubt starts to creep in again, but you need to ignore it.

Focus on the now, not the next. The next is filled with uncertainties that dampen the motivation you're riding right now. The next says hold back, think twice, play it safe. It tells

184

you to listen to everybody else and ignore yourself. It says stop moving.

You take a deep breath and close your eyes for a second before looking back to your champagne cork figure. Carefully, you pull at his limbs and straighten him up.

Each small tweak gives him a little more confidence. You think about yourself, perched on the edge of this old barrel, relishing in this feeling of anticipation without thinking too much about where it leads. You model the figure in your image, finally creating the perfect self-portrait. It's only then that you realise you've been sitting there for a while.

It's still quiet when you get back to the bar. The whole place has that emptiness that slows everything down. The occasional drinker drifts up to the bar, the beer trickles into the glass and floats back to the tables with barely a word.

Eventually, closing time rolls around and the last dregs filter out. The final wipe downs are finished, the glasses are thrown through the dishwasher, and it comes time to go home.

But first, you need to let them know that you're not coming back. You approach your manager and get his attention.

"I just wanted to let you know…"
"Hang on, before you…"

"It's been good and all but it's going to be…"

"I don't think this is really working out."

Well, at least that was easy. Short and sweet, not really working out. You can't say that you're disappointed, the outcome is the same, but it still stings a little. You've been robbed of your liberating exit and, instead, you've been given the boot.

You thank him, for some reason, and collect your last pay packet. The cold hits you hard as you leave and head towards the bus stop.

As you rifle through the notes in your hand, the next rears its ugly head again. It starts prodding at you with questions about how you're going to make money and what you're going to do if it all goes wrong. The unstoppable force is grinding to a halt.

As you march towards the bus stop, trying to outrun the wind, the buildings feel like they're closing in on you. The harsh stone and clinical lights suffocate you and you start panicking as you wonder if you'll ever get out.

The bus stop is empty when you arrive. You sit hunched over, staring into the ground, still clutching the thin brown envelope of cash. As you stuff it into your pocket, you feel your wire self-portrait.

Smile as you roll it around in your pocket and take it out, lifting it into the moonlight and admiring it. The thin wire falls out of focus as you look through it and see the piercing stars against the black sky. The next falls away and the now feels okay again.

DON'T TRUST A NEVER TRY

Don't stray off the path, don't step on the grass, do what signs say. It's okay to have a laugh from time to time but only after you've been stern and learned the right way to stay in line, on your long journey through time.

Remember to work and then play. You're born and told; you must prepare for when you're old.

Ambition and dreaming are great.

But in real life, does dreaming put food on your plate? Behave sensibly now or things will be ostensibly worse, and you'll curse yourself for not staying on course.

The woods off the path are harrowing, full of monsters and goblins with teeth like arrows, the terrain is never the same, impossible to map and full of dead dreams. You'll get lost and fall down a sink hole or cliff, just think once you're on your knees in submission how you'll regret trusting foolish ambition. Stay on the path, hide your dreams like a pin code to your soul. Don't use it frivolously, be miserly with it and when you look back, I'm sure you'll be happy to still have your dream in its vault, untouched, encased, safe and unattempted. Do not be tempted off the path.

People who don't try are so full of contempt and hatred for those that do. They're always content to crush whoever's dream they find while it's still young and undefined. Don't trust the never-trys that whisper these lies. Whisper back "I'll die on my feet before I concede defeat".

Nervous sweat gathers on your skin. It pools on your forehead and quietly drips down the curve of your cheek. Catch it in the crisp sleeve of the oversized blazer and shuffle into the hard seat.

Harsh lights burn overhead, baking the still air at a thousand degrees. Sweat stings the skin under your faded white shirt, gathering where your back touches the chair.

If it were up to you, you'd still be in your sweatpants and T-shirt, but it said clearly in the email, please wear office attire.

Slide a sheet off the desk and pretend to read the contents.

It's the same every time- Pretend to do work. Shuffle between in piles and out piles. Tap your fingers slowly over the keyboard. Make believe that you do any work here at all.

But today feels a little different, more proper somehow.

Rest your elbow on the smooth wooden surface and place your chin in your hands, like contemplating the incoherent mess on the page requires every ounce of your concentration.

A pair of high-heels click-click-clicks past the line of desks behind you, the other slouched bodies staring as she passes them by. She stops beside you, glancing at the blank monitor and vacant keyboard.

"Working hard I see."

Her arms cross, she stares at your damp expression.
You strain a smile...
but don't smile too much. This is a serious place of work, after all.
...it subsides and you mirror her stern reflection.
Drop the sheet on the desk and swivel the chair to face her. You have an excuse - one you've been rehearsing in your head for the last hour.

"I've just been going over these figures."

You motion to the sheet lying dormant on the desk.

"But something just doesn't add up."

She scoffs like it might be your fault, leans over and scans the page. Her expression dissolves as she looks over the numbers.

"Hmm."

She turns the sheet to face her and leans on the desk. This close, you see the confusion written across her brow.

"This makes no sense."

She moves around the desk, whipping the paper in the air and taking it with her. You feel the eyes of every other office lackey fall on the back of your head.

"55962502."

She lays the sheet down and looks over the reactions of the room. You drop your eyes, staring at the bright red fingernails resting on your desk.

"Whose account is that?"

Silence.
The air is frosted with the cold stare of the woman towering above you. Glance over your shoulder at the row of suits, your deflated doubles hunched behind the same desk, the same screen. No one can meet her eye.

"There's no use hiding."

She crosses her arms and walks down the row of desks.

"Two seconds is all I need to find out."

A familiar feeling washes over your skin, one you've not felt since school - scorn, like the entire office forgot to do their maths homework.

She tuts and sighs a bit too dramatically. Despite what every job says about new opportunities in life, it's always just another set of rules to learn. Sometimes you think you never really left school at all.

"Alright then."

She reaches the door at the side and rests her hand on the handle.

"Let's find out, shall we?"

You feel the tension lift as the door quietly opens. It doesn't slam shut or swing closed. It gently clicks like a child's bedroom door. Somehow it feels worse.

Turn and meet the other skittish eyes in the room. At the far end, a young guy in a navy suit stands and rushes out of the other door. Every eye in the room watches him go.

Stillness falls over each desk. One by one, you each hunch into the keyboards and start to type. Turn and fall into the solid back of the chair, eyes locked on the blank monitor.

Click.

The kettle rumbles to a close. Pour it in a mug and watch the steam drift above the counter. The door opens behind you and two guys in identical suits walk in with Sainsburys bags.

"Alright."

They mumble, almost in unison and take a seat at the small table.

Let onto them with a nod and continue making a brew. There's a quiet minute as they rustle inside their bags, burst open their cans and rip their sandwiches free. But the quiet feels tense somehow, like you were supposed to say something but didn't.

"Crazy what happened before."

One blurts through a mouthful of BLT.
The other nods whilst chewing then washes it all down with coke.

"Yeah."

He puts the food down and looks over his shoulder. You feel him take a second to wait for your reaction.

You should have offered them a brew, you think. Press the teabag on the side of the mug and toss it in the bin. It doesn't matter too much; they'd have said no anyway.

Pour the milk and slide it back into the fridge door. You fall in the seat and sigh. They both stop chewing and stare at you.

"What was it then?"
"What was what?"

You blow on the tea and take a sip.

"All of that before"

He splits a bag of crisps and chews open-mouthed.

"What had the new guy done?"
"Nothing major."

You inch the mug across the table and back again.

"Numbers were off, but not by much. It doesn't look good for him though."

They both nod and attack their sandwiches. Your eyes rest on the faded letters peeling from the mug.
Don't ta k t un il I'v ha my morni   coffee.
One of them finishes off the sandwich, looks around and leans into the table.

"This doesn't leave this room, right?"

He pauses for you both to nod along with the secrecy.

"And you didn't hear any of this from me."

He smiles to himself, revelling in the drama and attention over a deep breath. You cut through the pause.

"Go on then."
"So, the other morning my bus is running late, the whole way we're stuck behind this huge truck. Stop and start, the whole way."

He pushes his Coke to the side and leans his arms on the table.

"I get off a few stops earlier, figure if I run, I might not be too late."

The other guy starts back on his crisps, his short attention drifting from the table.

"Anyway, just as I'm coming past that Greggs, who should I see getting out of the Boss's car?"

His eyes pass between the two of you as he nods oh-so-knowingly. The crunch of crisps pauses from beside you, followed by a bewildered look.

"Who?"
"The new guy."
"Oh right."

He opens his mouth and shovels in more crisps.

"You reckon they're sleeping together?"
"Hundred percent."

The other one falls back in his chair.

"Just watch the way they look at each other."

You're not sure how to react...
...you need to be more shocked. This is news to you, remember?
...so you shake your head in disbelief.

"See I reckon that..."

He freezes as the door swings open. The boss stands there, one hand on the handle, the other gripping the frame. Despite her usual composed face, there's a glimmer of nerves hidden in the furrows of her brow. She locks eyes with you and sighs.

"Sorry, not who I was looking for."

She snaps the door closed. In her absence, they both pass the same told you so smile across the table. Your chair scrapes on the ground as you stand.

"Well, back to it, I guess."

They look a little confused as you open the door and exit with the tea in hand. Was there more you were supposed to say? You rack your brain but come up with nothing.

The door swings to a close behind you.

Click.

The same bodies line the row of desks, but there is something new in the air. Lights still roast your skin in sweat, a vacant mind rattling over the keyboard. But if you scratch beneath the quiet, you'd discover something else there.

A combination of intrigue and relief has settled across the office that, while there may be trouble ahead, at least they are not the responsible party. At least for now, everyone has managed to dodge a nasty bullet. Apart from the new guy.

Glance casually over your shoulder. At the back of the room, his is the only face that isn't buried deep in work. The clock ticks through a painful silence.

His shoulders hang as low as the expression he wears, moving only to heave a sigh into the indifferent space. Occasionally he will turn to face the boss's door like a dead man staring at the gallows, but for the most part, his eyes focus on some point a thousand miles away.

You notice one of your lunch partners take a quick glance at the condemned party. He catches your eye from across the room and gives you a nothing we can do shrug. Turn back to your keyboard.

Any minute now, the door to her office is going to open. Everyone knows that...

And when she comes, you need to be more scared. She is the boss, remember?

...it's just a matter of time.

Fill the passing seconds with hands that appear to type. If there's any skill you have in all of this, pretending to work is the greatest trick of all. They could give you any job, and you'd find a way to act like you're busy. You've become an expert at going through the motions, you've had plenty of practice.

Somewhere in the space behind you, whispers are exchanged. Shut your eyes and try pick out anything that might be about you. Under the low hum of the lights and occasional key tap or mouse click, you can't make out a single word.

Seconds pass into minutes. The office lights hum through the quiet shuffle of a dozen stiff suited bodies. From the other end of the room, the door gradually creaks open.

After her performance earlier, it's hard for everyone's eyes not to fall on her figure in the door frame, waiting for lightning to strike again. She announces to the room -

"Could I see you in my office, please?"

You turn to try and watch for the new guy's reaction. Instead, you find every lackey's dumb expression staring back at you. Turn and find her standing at your desk, arms crossed and face almost blank with emotion.

You don't say a word...

...just accept it. You don't know what's coming yet. Be a little nervous, but not too much....

...the chair scrapes on the wooden floor. She turns and walks into the dark of her office, and you follow. Sweat glimmers on your brow, coating the skin under the cheap plastic blazer in a visible display of discomfort.

Behind you, the door snaps shut, separating you from the identical rows of characters outside.

Click.

The high-backed seat raises her eyeline above yours, leaving her to stare down her nose at the crumpled suit drowning you. You straighten your back, lift your body to meet hers but her stare beats you back down.

Her question hangs in the air, the silence rippling across her pristine desk. A confused umm escapes your mouth. Roll your shoulders as your eyes dart about the blank office space for an answer.

"I don't understand"

You let the words linger there for a moment.

"This isn't my account."
"The thing is…"

She leans back on the chair, pushing her fingertips together in a steeple.

"Following the numbers back, all the accounts seem to point to you."

She spreads a small stack of pages on the wood. Your eyes fall over the gleaming white paper. Your mind falters, scrambling for the next thing to say…

…remember, purposeful silence is good. Just don't let it go on for too long.

…you break the pause with an explosive sigh and fall into the seat.

"But the error wasn't on my end."

The words return. Rearrange yourself in the hard seat and motion to the pages between you.

"I've done nothing wrong."

"As far as I'm concerned, you're the one who has broken company policy."

She weaves her fingers together and rests them on the desk.

"Rather than go through the rigmarole of an inquiry into the missing balance, the company would strongly suggest..."

She trails off, hoping her stern expression can finish the sentence.

"What are you saying?"

The words come louder now, something like anger cracking at the back of your throat.

"Am I being fired?"

Her eyes close and she composes herself over a deep breath.

"Look, between you and me..."

Her blue eyes pierce open, staring at you with a glimmer of sympathy.

"This is nothing personal. If you admit to the error and leave voluntarily, we can help you."

A forced smile spreads across her face, like she were an old friend offering advice.

"But if you decide to take this any further..."

The smile drops into her familiar glare and she shakes her head.

"The choice is yours."

"But it was the new guy who..."

"What he may or may not have done is not up for discussion."

She rises from her seat and curls two fists on the desk.

"The fact is you were responsible for the account. You're the one who broke the rules."

You feel the scene ending. Her words are final, like the finishing blow to an almost beaten boxer. It's your cue to stand and walk towards the door.

Pause for a moment with your hand on the handle. You are both frozen in your poses, unable to look each other in the eye.

But this is not the end for you. The last words are yours for the taking, a rebuttal from the man being pummelled against the ropes.

"Before I leave..."

You stop for effect. This is your final line, turn to her and make her really feel the gravity of your exit.

"I just want to wish you and the new guy the best of luck in your relationship."

The words feel like silk out of your mouth. Her eyes and jaw drop, confirming the staffroom rumours. Even though you were always going to lose this one, it feels good to get the last word in. You can't wipe the smile from your face.

Open the door and stare into the void outside the office.

"I'm sure you two will be very happy together."

Step into the darkness. The door clicks shut behind you.

And cut.

"Alright everyone, take five."

The voice calls from the front row. He claps his hands together, the sound ricocheting across the stage. ⸰There's plenty of notes and a lot for us to talk about today⸰

Coming in from the wings, you step around the door and into the office. There's a huge sense of relief as the rehearsal comes to a close. It's only a character but even acting the part makes you feel heavy. It would have been so easy to fall into a job like that and lose all momentum.

Your boss drops into the chair and slides her shoes off under the desk.

"I fucking hate high heels."

She leans back in the chair and shuts her eyes. Lifting a leg to the seat, she starts to massage her foot.

"We can swap if you want."

Take your blazer off and brush the sweat mixed into your hair.

"Might be a good addition to my character."

She lets out a tired chuckle and slumps deeper in the chair. She gives a half-hearted thumbs up.

"You did alright. Just keep working on your lines, yeah?"
"I will. Thanks."

You nod and look out across the stage.

The minimalist set-up means you can see from her office, across the row of desks and right through to the tiny cabinet feature in the staffroom. A few of the other office workers have stripped off their blazers and are walking into the empty rows of seats.

You hear the shuffle of wheels over the hard floor. The black shoes dangle from her hand as she starts to walk to the stairs at the front of the stage. She speaks over her shoulder.

"Get yourself a green tea and honey, it'll help your voice."

Clear your throat, feeling the dry skin burn under the piercing hot stage lights. Maybe you should get some on your way home, but more than anything you need something sweet and fizzy now.

The can bursts open as you sit by yourself in the dim aisles, looking over the stage. It's funny how much smaller it is from down here. You try picture yourself sitting at the desk, pretending to work while someone watches your every move.

The first time you were up there, it felt like there were lead weights in your shoes. But after months of rehearsals and not much else, you find yourself forgetting about everything outside of that strange, elevated space.

Working on this play puts a mirror up to an alternate version of you. What if you'd listened to all the advice, given up on all the so-called unrealistic ideas and taken the easy choice? You might be doing this for real. You could be playing the part of an office worker in a real office instead of on stage. You're so glad you didn't trust the people that were afraid to try. Pretending to be them is enough for you.

"Hey."

The teacher slinks down the aisle and shuffles into the empty seat beside you.

200

"Can I just run through some feedback with you?"
"Sure."

You lean back and smile.

He pushes back the fringe of his dark black hair and begins flicking through frantic marks in a small leather notebook. While his eyes rush over the pages, he nods his head and mumbles - right right right.

In a row of seats at the far end of the stage, your boss sits with two of the office workers and the writer. Each of them slouches low in a chair, their feet dangling over the seats in front.

"So, first things first."

His heavy-set eyes move from the pages and settle on you.

"You did a decent job. I really did believe that you were in that office."
"Thanks"

You smile and breathe a little easier. His finger brushes down the lines of scrawls in his tiny notebook.

"What else... Ah, now you smile a lot."

He lifts his face to reveal an almost wrinkled, smoke-stained smile. It fades and he motions to the stage.

"But don't smile too much. This is a serious place of work, after all."

WHITE HORSES SONG

*The road ahead looks dark, an impossible task for a child
wearing an adult mask. I'll focus on the first step of a
million more to where I don't know but I'll get there fast
or slow.*

*My friends race on white horses, shore bound, and I look
on treading water, splashing around, as the list of life's
meaning is burning short, I swear not to drown before
my real life is found.*

*My intentions are good but its action that pays for food
and I need to make a move to escape a losers fate, I have
no time to wait, I hope I'm not too late.*

*When my friends race on white horses, shore bound, and
I look on treading water, splashing around, as the list of
life's meaning is burning short, I swear not to drown
before my real life is found.*

*My pen and paper dream could see me free of my
personality and come out clean. Now I know I'm not an
artist, I've never been the smartest but if I keep on when
the rest get bored, just maybe, I'll catch a shore wave
reward.*

*I can race white horses, shore bound, and I won't be
treading water, not splashing around, and my life's
meaning will be burning forth. Yes, I won't drown,
because my real life is found.*

It's been almost a year since you first stepped into an acting
class on a whim. You still don't really know why you decided to

go, but you're glad you did. There was never a sense that it was going to be your calling or anything like that, it was just one of those things you did. A year on, you're still going and the idea of it being something real doesn't seem so far off anymore.

You step into the icy streets and steady yourself for a moment, thinking about where to go next. The class is done with, and you haven't got anything else planned until the next one.

It's been a year, falling from job to job, searching for something to sustain you while you worked out where you were going long term. The acting and writing are fun, but you still need a 'proper job, 'as people call it. As if nobody gets paid to be an actor.

So, you ended up jumping from random idea to madcap suggestion while your passions ticked over in the background.

But it didn't feel so hopeless anymore. You might not have loved the jobs and maybe you got fired from more than a few, but they didn't feel like a sinkhole you were trying to escape from.

There was always that other thing to grasp onto. Whatever job you were working was just to keep you going until your true purpose materialised and you managed to grab hold of it.

You check the time, it's only mid-afternoon. The rest of the week stretches out ahead of you, filled with a few dull job applications, the occasional pint with a mate but, mainly, a whole lot of dead time to kill.

Check your phone, even though you know that there won't be any messages. All your pals are at work for another few hours at least, staring at computers or pissing people off with unwanted phone calls. You've done all that and it wasn't for you, so you're back to finding ways to fill dead space until the next thing comes along.

At the start, it felt alright. It's always an uphill struggle if you want to do something exciting with your life, and the people that make it are just the ones that stick at it.

But now it's starting to drag a bit and it's a lot harder to stay positive when you're skint and bored all day while everybody else is on a direct track towards something. Even if that something looks like your worst nightmare.

Whenever you talk to people about it, there's always the thing left unsaid. They say it's inspiring that you're following your passion but they're holding back that golden question; what happens if it doesn't work out?

Don't take it personally though, it's not a reflection on you. It's not that they don't believe you, they just can't imagine living so fiercely in the present without a backup plan in place. It's admirable, but it scares them.

You roll it all around in your head and find yourself wandering aimlessly. A thin drizzle coats your face and sits on top of your hair without soaking in.

There was talk of snow last week, but it never appeared. Just a blanket of grey and damp that's lasted for days. Sometimes you wish that it would just make its mind up. Either rain or don't, this middle ground is getting tedious now.

Suddenly, you find yourself at a bus stop. Not your normal one, you don't know where the buses go from here. There's an old couple hunched over on the bench, shielding from the spray as they wait, eyes fixed at some point down the road.

You don't know why, but you just sit down. The old lady smiles and you smile back. You wonder what they used to do before they spent their days trying to fill the time just like you.

It's a good ten minutes until a bus arrives. Sit there, watching cars roll by, kicking up a spray from the damp road. The drivers stare ahead, following the road automatically. Going through the motions without thinking about the why of it all.

Is that what happens as people get older? Any semblance of meaning or direction slowly dissolves as each day chips away at ambition and then one day, you're just doing what you do without knowing if it's what you really want.

That won't happen to you. You've found the things that you're passionate about and for a while, it helped. But the road ahead is starting to look murky.

Everybody around you knows what they're doing and you feel like you're just treading water, and it's getting harder.

Eventually, a bus pulls up. The old couple get up and board as the doors hiss open. They buy their tickets and take a seat near the front. You didn't hear where they said they were going but you jump on and ask the driver for the same.

The empty bus is a tired relic that will continue running twice a day for a few years until the last remaining passengers move on and the service is retired.

You take a seat at the back and shuffle around, trying to get comfortable on the scratchy seats. The old couple are at the front, silent but comfortable. You don't really stop to think about where you're going, you just enjoy the sensation of rolling along, listening to the rain drumming against the windows.

The sharp air comes through the cracks in the rickety old bus and nips at every unprotected spot on your body. Pull your coat in tighter and turn away from the window. Take out your headphones and put some music on. You can afford to shut your eyes for a minute.

****

The bus hits a bump in the road and jolts you awake. Come to your senses. The lingering memory of a dream sends anxiety shooting through your body. You can't pick out the details, you just have an image.

You're stuck in the water, thrashing around and trying to reach the surface. Every time you briefly break through the waves, your friends and family stand on the shore, slowly moving away from you.

Shake the image and stretch out a bit, looking around to see where you are. The city is long gone and you're on a country road somewhere. The hills stretch out as far as you can see, blurred by the never-ending sheet of half-rain. The old couple from before are gone, it's just you on the bus.

Maybe the driver never noticed you missed your stop or maybe he just didn't care. It winds along the narrow road for another few minutes while you stare out of the window, picking out the occasional sheep in the hills.

Up ahead, you see the beginnings of a village and, eventually, pull up at a small bus stop outside a quaint little shop. A few locals push on towards home with their heads down and coats wrapped tightly around them.

A woman and her young boy get onto the bus and pay up. She smiles at you as she takes a seat a few rows ahead. The bus pulls away again and you go back to staring out of the window.

After a while, you take your phone out and start rifling through the notes. Smile to yourself as you read over some of the ideas you tapped out over the last couple of weeks.

There's a good rhythm to some of the words and the images. As you revisit them, making tweaks here and there, you start feeling a bit more energetic. There's something in them. Sure, they're not perfect but you can see them improving over time.

Open a blank page and start typing, thinking back to your dream, locked in the water. Something new starts to take shape as you put the mental back and forth of the day in words. You write for a while until you hit a natural stopping point and the phone goes back in your pocket.

Push yourself up in the seat and look out of the window again. The clouds are starting to clear slightly and a thin ray of damp sun cuts across the hills. The small village is a dot in the distance by this point.

Green slopes rise in front of you, and you still don't give much thought to where you are or where you're going. For now, you're just enjoying being on the bus with the countryside around you and your adult obligations somewhere far behind you. It's peaceful as you rest your head against the window and drift in and out of sleep.

Your eyes flicker open and closed and you half watch the young kid and his mum sitting further up the bus. His head is buried in his mum's phone, playing some game with flashing colours and jerky animations.

Such a simple thing has his full attention, with nothing to drag him away. Nothing else exists apart from his game. You miss the feeling, maybe that's why you got on the bus in the first place.

It's an opportunity to revert to childhood, making decisions on a whim and doing whatever you feel like doing in the moment. No need to think about where the road leads or what could go wrong along the way. You smile to yourself and drift off again.

****

A huge wave crashes over your head and drags you towards the bottom. You fight hard to burst above the swell, sucking in as much air as you can before the next wave throws you under again.

Through salt-stung eyes, you see flashes of white on the shore. The panic is setting in and every attempt to reach the surface is getting harder. The water hammers down on you and you're thrown around like a rag doll. As the fear grips, you're waving your arms wildly, getting nowhere.

But then you stop and close your eyes. Let the panic subside as the waves drag you back and forth. Slowly kick your legs and drag your arms through the water, following the crest of the waves. Don't let your nerve break as the water washes over you. Progress is slow but you're moving gradually towards the shore. As you get closer, you spot the white shapes again-

You're dragged from your dream by a gentle shaking on your arm. It's the woman and her son. You sit up quickly, embarrassed, and look around.

"End of the line, love."

She smiles at you and turns to get off the bus. You grab your bag and rush out into the street. As you step off, you hear seagulls screeching in the distance somewhere. The smell of fried doughnuts and chips hits you and you suddenly realise how hungry you are. You look around and see the ocean in the distance, thrashing in the sharp wind.

It's a grey day and the place is deserted. You see the woman and her son wandering off into the distance. Check that you haven't left anything on the bus and wait for it to pull away. Then, head towards the sea.

When you get to the front, you see a long stretch of metal shutters. Tacky gift shops and arcades, all hibernating until the summer rolls around and they open again, trying desperately to eek a living out of the small handful of tourists that still come here.

You wonder what it was like fifty years ago. Shops with generations of the same family, never wondering what they're going to do because they've always known. Father teaches son the ropes and he takes over when he's ready.

But what now? The life they've always known is fading away and suddenly everything is clouded. Generations of meaning and purpose disappear in a matter of decades.

You run your fingers along the shutters as you walk, the paint peels away and floats down towards the beach. At the end, you spot a few lights and see a couple of people milling about. You haven't eaten since breakfast and you're starting to feel it.

The chippy at the end is still open, staying afloat off the back of the locals. You check your wallet, hoping to find some notes, but it's empty. Rummage around in your jacket pocket and feel the weight of a few pound coins.

Count them out and then head inside to see what you can afford. Just enough for a sausage and chips.

The soft batter, soaked in grease slides down your throat and warms you from the inside out. The chips are a little dry and limp, but they fill a hole. Sit on the wall above the beach, watching seagulls circle the deep green water as you eat. A drink would wash it down nicely, but you don't have enough cash left.

You think about all your mates, getting their own flats and heading out to the pub every weekend while you're at home, counting the pennies and struggling to find enough for a can of Coke.

Would it have been easier if you stuck it out at Uni or just knuckled down at one of the many jobs you've quit over the last year? At least you'd have your own space by now.

You're an actor, can't you just play the part of average man with a boring job? Get up, go to work, come home, eat, sleep, repeat. The lines are easy to learn, but you know how hard it is to make it convincing.

Everybody around you seems to nail it but the idea of living a false life doesn't sit right with you.

Throw the translucent, slimy paper into the bin and hop down onto the beach. It's getting late and you need to head back soon. But first, you want to get as far away as you possibly can.

The wet sand slips under your feet as you make your way towards the sea. The wind picks up a chill from the water and cuts through to your bones. The beach is deserted apart from a couple of dog walkers in the distance.

You reach the edge of the water and watch the thin foam slide in and out over the stones. As the rough water churns, you find yourself thinking back to the hardest times in your life. The times when you put a smile on and, 'everything's fine ' became a catch phrase.

At least your life had purpose then, you were working towards a degree, a job, a normal life. But all you had was purpose and no meaning. You didn't know who you were and finding out seemed impossible.

Take your shoes and socks off and push your feet into the ground, curling your toes into the sand. Your skin turns a bright shade of white and goes numb. Roll your trousers up and take a few steps out, letting the water lap gently against your legs.

Close your eyes and you're back out there again, trapped in the icy waters. Your friends are on the shore, racing on white horses, leaving you behind.

The waves are getting rougher, and you're being dragged further from the shore.

But determination is keeping you afloat. You might not have all the answers now and maybe things won't work out the way that you hoped they would, but that's not what's important.

There's no need to race, just keep pushing forward. Relax and let the waves carry you and when you can, swim.

Progress may be slow but you're still moving in the right direction. It's only the people that stop swimming who drown. They give up and let the waves wash over them, pulling them towards the bottom.

But you just keep kicking along. Every now and again, a wave catches you just right and drives you further towards the shore. Your friends in the distance are getting closer, the waters becoming calmer. The sun breaks through the clouds and you feel a slight warmth on your face. Stretch your legs towards the bottom and you can almost feel sand. Just a little bit further.

You open your eyes and realise you can't feel your feet. Check the time, you need to get back before the last bus leaves without you.

It's hard not to smile as you run for the bus, your shoes half laced up. You're not trying to force yourself into anybody else's idea of what your life should look like. Now you're going after the things that you're excited about, even if it's not the safe option.

You know who you are now, at least you think. And that's good, it's going to be important.

PART III

The bottom of the glass is visible now.

I can see it bending and changing in the light.

Endings are never really clear. They shift constantly, and sometimes disappear completely.

How do I find clarity?

It will find you, when you least expect it.

IS SHIT LUCK FOLLOWING ME?

I can still remember last December, when everything seemed like it would last forever but since then I've been peppered with misfortune hitting like bad weather on my holidays, this is not why I paid.

Shit luck again for me, uni drop out, didn't get his degree, and not a job that I didn't leave, but this year it's cancer for me, which is really just too much, can I get some luck?

Looking back, it's all been good prep, for not tripping on the next uneven step. I hope you see the luck that's hiding from me behind the bins or a barn, cactus or tree. You take it and keep it away, I'm still enjoying my day to day. That will never change.

I'll build a house in my family tree so they're always there just around me.

It won't shake and the wind doesn't come through the leaves. It's a perfect palace, at the exact right time for me.

So I guess if I took the time to look I would see, that it's not misfortune spooning with me. My luck isn't running out, not while my friends and family are about.

My luck burns at 1000 degrees it shows me where to go and makes tanning a breeze. If it changed now, I'd be dropped to my knees because we'll see it through, together we can't lose.

A buzzing catches your ear. Look up at the fluorescent strip light and see a fly, darting around and crashing against the blue glow of the bulb. You watch it for a while, flying away before rapidly changing course and smashing back into the light.

It seems like an eternity passes while you follow its course, but it's only been a few minutes.

215

Outside, you can hear the cacophony of noise as the moving parts of the hospital rush back and forth. The swish and rattle of curtains being pulled back as doctors and nurses run from one patient to the next, following the beep and click of machines you'll never understand.

Beyond that, the faint nervous chatter from the waiting room. Look around at the murky green walls and steel tables. Shift your weight and try to get a bit more comfortable as you perch on the end of the bed.

Attempt to distract yourself with the informational posters on the wall but all you can see is the doctors face. They usually have a calming nature about them. No matter what the situation, doctors always stay level-headed. It's their job to reassure you while you panic.

When you came in, you thought it'd be a quick in and out.

Maybe you'd get a prescription, or it's one of those things that will pass on its own in a few days.

But the doctor's face suggested otherwise. A sense of urgency crept through the room as he called a nurse to begin a series of tests.

And it seemed like such a small thing- A numb hand.

You noticed it a week earlier and didn't think much of it.

People assume that it's always painful or you'll just collapse one day - but it all started without any of that. Just a numb hand.

Then, when the headaches kicked in, dad told you to go to the hospital. He was probably more worried than anyone, but he didn't want to let on, hoping that it would be nothing at all.

Things moved quickly once you arrived here. You told them about your symptoms and the mood changed in a second.

Usually, they take their time and just explore things a bit. It's a list of questions about lifestyle or diet and how much you exercise. But this time, you could tell that this wouldn't be a routine visit.

You sit there alone, legs dangling over the edge of the bed like a child. In a few hours, fate managed to put your whole life on pause.

And all you can think about is every wasted second- The stacks of hours spent in inertia, and the days spent wishing it was all different.

But you shouldn't regret a moment of it. The hard times teach you how to deal with the unexpected, and that's going to be a useful skill right now.

Eventually, the doctor comes back and tells you that they need to do a lot of tests. Something is happening, they just don't know what.

Call mum and dad. The voices down the line sound so strange to you. Even your own voice, the words you use are alien coming out your mouth.

After a while, they arrive and you all sit there, everybody afraid to talk. The tense silence is occasionally punctuated with attempts at reassurance, but nobody really believes it.

It's hard to say you think of anything in this time. It all happens so fast that you don't really have time to be scared. You're just stunned into feeling nothing.

When the tests come back, they tell you that there's a mass in your brain.

Mass. It's such a vague word, just a lump. A thing in your brain that shouldn't be there. Nobody really knows what it means yet, but it all starts feeling a lot more real.

Mum and dad start letting themselves worry, but you're still floating along, detached from the whole thing.

It's like you're watching yourself from above. Everything feels like a dream, slowly unfolding in front of you but you're not scared because it's just a picture in your head.

Even though you're at the centre of this terrifying revelation, your first thought is always for everybody else. You're desperate to hold everybody together because you know that if you fall down, everybody else will collapse in on themselves. You can't let that happen.

Lives come and go around you in the waiting room. Patients are seen, treated and sent on their way, ready to be replaced by the next one. In the constantly revolving machine, you stay still, waiting for more news. Everybody loses track of time as the minutes drag into hours.

The rest of the family rallies around you. They all try to put a brave face on things, looking away from the stark reality in front of them.

Then, more test results come back.

****

Those scenes in films and TV shows where people get bad news always seem so unrealistic. They sit there, zoning out and the doctor fades into the background, talking away.

Then a close up of their face as a shrill ringing sound drowns out the talking. Eventually, the doctor stops and waits for a response but the person just sits there for a minute until somebody shakes them back into the room. They missed it all, they stopped listening when they heard that one fateful word-cancer.

218

You used to think that it was all creative license and in real life, that's not how it would go. Surely there would be a

reaction. You'd be angry at how unfair it all was, terrified of what was to come, distraught because you knew that your loved ones were about to go through the most difficult period in their lives. But it played out just like it does on screen.

It didn't so much hit you as lifted you right out of your skin.

So you sit there, numb- unable to process what you've just

heard. It can't be real- this is the kind of thing that happens to other people.

It's easy to focus on how unfair it all seems. Aren't you due a bit of good luck? The last few years as a dropout in a series of dead-end jobs, you fought hard to find happiness and contentment.

And it felt like you were finally on the right track. Life was a future of possibilities, and you had the momentum to carry

you through. Now you've hit a brick wall and everything is

falling apart again. Where's the justice in that?

When all the tests are done with and there's nothing left to do for the night, you eventually get to go home. On the drive back, the situation still hasn't materialised. You're leaving it

all behind in the hospital like you've just woken up from the dream and none of it really happened.

You pull into the driveway and everybody slowly gets out and goes inside. The family walks through to the kitchen and you stand there in the dark, cautiously talking through what just happened. You're like shellshocked soldiers, recounting the traumas of battle, knowing that you only have a matter of hours before you're back on the front lines and things are only going to get harder.

That's what this is, a battle. The family is a unit and you're their commander. You know that you have to keep morale up and hold everybody together. You could sit there and think about how unfair it is. You could be angry that you're hit with shit luck when you've already had your fair share but that won't get you anywhere.

Instead, you all look ahead and start thinking about how you're going to fight this thing together. When you refuse to let bad luck rule you, things start moving.

Within a matter of days, dad is pulling strings and you've got the best surgeons on your case. It's a lot of consultations and conversations about what can be done. Specialist equipment is brought and plans are made, but things are still uncertain.

If you had time to stop and think, you might have been more scared. In the brief moments between the trips back and forth to the hospital, the whole family gathers, trying to stay positive.

You had every right to break down and get angry or sad or confused, but you didn't. The last few years of your life prepared you for this.

All the difficult times were training for the bigger challenges that were to come. Without that, who knows how you would have coped with this. Your instant reaction was to think that you had shit luck but the days after the diagnosis shifted your perspective.

When you looked around and saw your family by your side, going to the ends of the earth to help you fight, your luck was bought into focus. Whatever life throws at you, you've still got them.

Don't focus on the bad luck, let it shine a light on the things that will carry you through. Let it shield you from the harsh winds and see that, no matter what happens, you can't lose.

But still, there's uncertainty ahead. All the greatest medical minds in the world with all the best equipment can't tell you exactly what's going to happen.

They're going to open you up and cut a part of your brain out. The doctors have been upfront about it with you from the beginning. You could wake up blind or unable to move, or you might not make it through at all. The aftereffects could be for life, or they could pass. There's no way to tell and, for the first time, the fear starts setting in.

You're truly plunging yourself into the unknown and putting your fate in the hands of the surgeons. Life beyond that operating room is a blank and you won't find out what it looks like until you get to the other side.

The day finally arrives and you pack up to drive to the hospital. Stare out of the car window as you silently drive down familiar roads. A whole life's worth of memories, good and bad.

You think about all the time you spent putting a brave face on while you were lost at sea. Unrealistic expectations and the fear of disappointing people dragging you from day to day. Years of your life were spent going through the motions and doing what was expected instead of doing what you wanted.

Now, looking at all those memories rush by, you can't help but think you should have acted sooner. There was always the assumption that you had plenty of time, but now you're not so sure.

You can't be sure of anything anymore. If you could go back, you'd shake yourself and make yourself see that you were lucky all along, you were just blind to it.

The journey to the hospital feels like it goes on for hours. You arrive and park up. The place is packed with people, all locked inside their own heads, oblivious to the world around them. You're the same, floating along in a daze towards the doors. It's all starting to feel scarily real, it's no longer a dream that you'll wake up from soon. It's a harsh, random reality that you might not wake up from.

Mum and dad walk you through the doors and into the waiting room. Approach the desk and let them know you're here, and you're told to sit down and wait.

The cold, rigid chair digs into your back. There's no way you can get comfortable right now anyway. You look around at your family and everybody sits in stunned silence. There's nothing good to say.

You're gripped by fear but you don't want to let on. You don't want to start a domino effect that ripples through the family. If you can stay strong then it's easier for everybody else to bury the intense fear that they feel, but honestly you want to scream. Mum senses this and reaches across to hold your hand.

The clock ticks by slowly as you see people being called in and heading through the doors into the back. Focus on your breathing and try to shut out the anxiety screaming through your body as you wait for your name to be called. Mum squeezes your hand tight and sniffs.

Worst case scenarios and imagined futures force themselves into your head. You run through it over and over, wondering how the family will cope if something goes wrong. What if you come out of the other side changed forever? Are you prepared for your life to be different?

You don't have a choice though, and you know that. This is your only chance, so you just have to let go and hold onto hope. Hope that it goes as well as it can.

Mum places her other hand on top of yours, she stares at them, hardly blinking. A brief calm comes over you as you let go of the anxiety. All the speculating comes to a halt as you realise that you have no control over the situation anymore. It's all down to the surgeons and, to a large extent, luck.

There it is again, luck. The last week has been driven by it. The bad luck that put you in this waiting room in the first place, and the amazing luck of the people around you. All the random events of the last few years proved that you could get through anything as long as you have the right people.

Finally, your name is called. You all look at each other, unsure what to say. Hug your family tight, nobody wants to let go in case this is the last time.

You're taken into a cubicle and the curtain is drawn across so you can get changed. As soon as the swish of fabric cuts you off from your family, you feel lonelier than you ever have before. Half-naked, you feel the nurse on the other side of the curtain, waiting for you to get changed into your gown.

The scratchy, translucent material feels cold against your skin. You feel exposed and half wish you could just hide behind this curtain forever. But you know that you can't.

Eventually, you need to pull the curtain back. After you get changed, it's more waiting and lots of questions. It's probably a good thing you couldn't eat before you came in because you might have been sick if there was anything in your stomach.

The whole time the nurses are trying to reassure you and keep you calm as they go through the final checks. The surgeon comes to talk you through the procedure for the final time. Before you go in, you see your family again. Seeing you standing there in your gown for the first time brings the whole situation into focus.

One by one they wish you the best of luck. They all hold your hand or squeeze your shoulder- see you on the other end, they say.

You're taken to a bed and told to climb on, your arms awkwardly hanging by your side. You don't know what to do with your hands. The bright fluorescent lights sting your eyes. Crane your neck and look around as nurses prepare syringes and switch on machines.

In the sterile hum of the room, you are vulnerable and exposed to them all. The nurse works away, chatting to you about the weather and trying to take your mind off the life changing ordeal you're about to go through. You appreciate the effort, but it doesn't work.

She asks you to lie still while she takes your arm. Look away but feel the scratch and pull of the needle as it pierces in. You look back and see the small plastic bit sticking out of your arm, secured with a few pieces of tape.

The needle shifts inside your arm as you move around on the bed. The nurse takes a small syringe and draws in a milky liquid as the bed is wheeled out into the centre of the room.

Just past your feet, you can see the big double doors into the operating theatre. You wonder what they're thinking on the other side as they prepare to open your skull and remove the mass from your brain.

The nurse takes the syringe and injects the anaesthetic into your arm. She tells you to count back from ten, nine, eight, seven...

You feel the grogginess wash over you. Things slow down and you feel your eyes getting heavier.

In that moment, you reach out in your head and grab hold of an image of your family. The fear tries to break through as you lose consciousness and fight to keep your eyes open.

Five, four, three... Let the fear dissipate. Shit luck might have gotten you here in the first place, but the best luck in the world will get you out of the other side.

Two, one, zero...

MUM

Twenty twenty, which used to suggest perfect clarity are now synonyms with uncertainty. I still remember last Hogmanay with a family bonfire, drinking and revelry, all my plans seemed so clear, I had no idea we were all at the gates of a resolution cemetery.

The world began to shrink from global to national, cities to local and finally to home. It would be understandable in a world with no control for the mood to get really low. We all needed a hero.

That's where you came in to rescue our family sanity by providing a sanctuary. It's like you seemed to know it would be needed, like you had the gift of prophecy and saw the catastrophe on its way and said "no! We will ride it out in luxury". You took a cave and turned it into a place people will save to stay, and that we got to sit out the storm there for free, a gift that is not lost on me.

It's for things like this that you are the keystone of our family and always a rock for me personally. To have you so on my side that your love never leaves my periphery, is one of the things that will see me through anything.

I know it wasn't always easy and no one embraces a bad day like you do, but remember I've never known a bad day that isn't fixed by being embraced by you, and being reminded I'm one of the lucky few who hit the parental lottery jackpot and won a lifetime supply of calling you mum.

The afternoon wastes away outside, the low sun a mere flicker in the gathering dark. You stare out of the window at the wind thrashing through the hazy treetops. The sky threatens rain. A car's headlights flash through the icy cold, a familiar sight that looks so strange to you now.

Blink back into the room, with the TV droning through the quiet of the house. Each breath is heavy, dragging all the air deep into your lungs and releasing it with force.

Your head presses back and you try to sink deeper into the armchair, letting the soft leather swallow you. It doesn't work so you sit there, still under the weight of the dim living room, the crushing news in the background.

It wasn't that long ago that you danced through here. Last Hogmanay, drunk as anything with a brother under each of your arms. Jumping and thrashing in the air, the music drowned by the sound of the huddle's hoarse singing.

The year ahead felt like it held so much promise then, like a calm pool before a waterfall. As you tumbled into the new year, there was a dim sense of direction ushering you to follow over the waters end.

"...Fires continue to rage across the countryside..."

You blink and focus your good eye on the screen, the other half of the room filled with dim shadows. Images of wildfires ripple from the TV, casting a warm glow on the wall behind you. Lift your hand over half of your face and try to pick out the image of a burning forest through the noise of your right eye.

It's better than before, but still doesn't offer much. You shift your blurred vision across the room and settle on the light pouring in from the window.

Everything that was once familiar is now hidden in a veil of shadows. The world you knew so well before is a mere speck on the road behind you. What's worse is that you don't know if it will ever go back to normal.

It seems the new year did not bring the waterfalls you hoped for but rapids, the unforgiving water throwing your body from rock to rock and washing you up in this ancient armchair.

Nuzzle your head into the leather, the patch around the scar still numb, aside from the occasional throbbing. Given the options of waking up half blind and not at all though, you consider this the best result.

Convince your body to sit up. It's an effort, but using your good arm, push yourself a little straighter in the chair. Your other hand lies numb on the leather armrest. Tap out the fingers in sequence.

1, 2, 3.

1, 2, 3.

More than anything, you want control back.

The room has started to turn dark. What used to be a simple act of getting up and turning the light on has become a weighted decision. You break it down into stages.

Get up from the chair.

Balance yourself.

Walk to the switch and back.

Carefully drop to the seat.

Life is now a series of operations, minor tasks diffracted into their components and assessed in minutia. You reach out for the water, faithfully at your side on a small table to soothe your constantly dry throat.

Take a deep breath and shuffle your body to the edge of the chair. Count to three. Use your one good hand to propel your body upright. The walls turn as the blood inside your head rushes and eventually settles.

"...in a statement earlier today, the Health Secretary assured..."

Open your eyes, your body buried in the armchair again. It's hard to tell how long has passed.

An hour. Two. Maybe it's closer to a couple of weeks or a month. You can't tell.

Through one bleary eye, you're confronted by the pale and gaunt face of some balding man plastered on the screen. He's sat in his house somewhere, suit on and a microphone jutting from his oversized headset. Over the presenters drawn out question, he nods his head and interrupts.

"...the truth is at this point we don't truly understand the..."

Unconsciously, your head starts to nod in tandem with him.

You feel like a parrot. No, in fact it's worse than that. You feel like a mime. Stuck in this armchair, responding with vaguely human gestures, the voice lodged somewhere inside your throat.

The rattle of cutlery from the other room catches you off guard. If you had more energy, you'd jump in the seat. Shut your eyes and try to focus on who it is.

Normally you can tell who is doing what from the sound alone - Mum is heavy handed in the kitchen, but light-footed anywhere else in the house. Dad is a little more delicate, even his rare laughter a silent chesty motion rather than a sound.

Your brothers on the other hand are a storm wherever they go. The three of you are indistinguishable like that, at least you used to be. As the kettle begins to rumble over the clink of mugs, you figure it must be...

"Love"

Mum bellows from the kitchen, her slippered feet moving silent through the hallway.

"Do you fancy a cup of tea?"

She pauses by the door, waiting for a response while half watching the screen. Her arms cross as she leans on the frame, the presenter standing in front of a large rising graph.

"Yeah. Thanks."

Your voice is raspy. Your good hand lunges for the water, knocking the glass over to thud on the soft rug. A puddle spreads through the fabric, turning the dark blue material grey.

"Shit."

You lean forward on the chair, blinking at the spill.

"Don't worry about it."

She reassures you, stepping across the room and picking up the glass.

"I'll get you another."
"I'll go for a vodka this time. Neat."

You smile and give a thumbs up.

Her laughter is fitting for a joke far funnier than what you came out with. It's become the new norm.

There are enough bad things in this situation to fill a hundred lists, and this seems trivial, but it's been on your mind for a while now - Mum and Dad keep laughing too hard at your jokes.

It was charming at first. For a bit you even thought you'd come out the other side of this a funnier person. But after two days in the house, trying purposefully to be unfunny, you learnt the value of a good joke and what constitutes real laughter.

There was a glimmer of worry when you first worked it all out, like the rest of your life would be a string of people humouring you. But you can see it for what it is now- every pretend laugh is just as much for them as it is you, a saving grace in an otherwise shit situation. We all need a hero sometimes.

In the other room, you hear the clatter of mugs and the faint whine of the tap. You've no idea where the others are, but they can't have gone far. Not now at least.

"...A leading figure for the economic think tank has suggested that those hit hardest will..."

The cold stare of the presenter starts to drain what little energy there was in the room. You know the remote is nearby, but is it worth searching for?

Mum slinks into the room and lays the drinks on the small table beside you.

"Thanks."

You smile and raise the cup to your lips, shakily sipping at it.

Mum rests a hand on her hip as the TV pulls her attention in. She stands tall beside you, the presenter's monotone and proper voice forcing the world outside into the calm space of the living room. She looks over her shoulder.

"Is there nothing else on?"

"Eh, I'm not really watching it."

Press your back into the seat and stretch both arms in front of you.

"Just background noise."

She nods and leaves. Your hands fall to the armrest and you sigh into the vacant room, wondering what to do next.

Only boring people get bored.

Mum said that a lot when you were kids. Not that you were ever truly bored back then, you realise that now. Sometimes it was just an excuse to get her attention. In fact, it was nearly always that.

Well, why don't you go play with your brothers?

If you could, you would.

You imagine the three of you out in the garden, passing a rugby ball between you, running from one end to the other while ducking and weaving between their tackles.

Stretch your legs as high as you can, dipping your toes forward and slowly rolling them back. The idea of running seems almost foreign to you now. Kind of like when you have a cold, you forget what breathing through your nose even feels like. It's a drastic comparison to your situation, but one that you can't shake from your thoughts.

Force out a yawn and start to tap your fingers on the leather, your good hand mirroring the pattern of the other.

1, 2, 3, 4.

1, 2, 3, 4.

Curl both hands into fists, release and repeat.

"...as cases continue to rise..."

The screen snaps to black. In the dark reflection, your mum stands with the remote in one hand and a cup of tea in the other.

"Think that's enough for one day."

She glides across the rug, sitting on the sofa beside you. Kicking her slippers off, she curls her legs underneath and sighs into the room.

"Dinner shouldn't be long. Just need to wait on the others."

Outside, the rain starts to push through dark clouds. Wind gathers through the trees as large drops splatter on the window, slowly trickling into a downpour.

Everyone else is upstairs, locked into their computers in makeshift offices, screens filled with tiny portals into the homes of colleagues.

As the world started to shrink, Mum made sure the house expanded to accommodate everyone. Your brother brought his growing family along, staying at the guest house at the end of the garden. Even dad was sure to work from home whenever he could.

You push yourself to the edge of the seat and turn to face mum out of your one good eye.

"Spoken to anyone today?"

She rolls her eyes.

"Well, I spoke to your gran's forehead for a while."

You force a chesty laugh and lean back into the armchair.

"I tell her every time, hold the phone further away but it never works."

Mum blows on her tea and takes a sip.

"She's doing well though. Said she's missing everyone."

You nod and start to tap your finger's out in sequence again.
1, 2, 3.
1, 2, 3.

"We should do a big quiz or something."

Turn your head and look out the window as trails of rain freefall down the glass.

"If everyone isn't sick of them at this point."

Mum laughs and wraps her hands around the mug.

"If your uncle beats Dad again, I don't think I'll ever hear the end of it."
"He's not still going on about that, is he?"
"Oh, you know what those two are like."

She shakes her head.

An alarm starts beeping from the kitchen. Mum uncurls herself from the seat, slides her feet in the slippers and springs upright.

"That'll be dinner."

She half rushes out of the room, shouting over her shoulder.

"I'll get the others then we're good to go."

Your eyes fall across the room and settle on the ground. The alarm cuts off from the kitchen and you hear the oven open, the roar of whatever is roasting fills the house. The smell drifts into the living room and fills your mouth with drool.

If this were a cartoon, your body would be lifted by that smell. You would dangle by your nose on a trail of the scent, drifting out of the room and settling at the table with an oversized bib on, knife and fork ready in hand.

You don't know what's for dinner, all you know is that you need a lot of it.

Take a sip of water, grip the arm rest and shuffle to the edge of the seat. Breathe in and out. Count to three. Heave yourself to your feet.

Freeze as the room stops turning, hold your arms out ready to catch yourself. It subsides and you breathe into the room again.

You've never been so aware of your body, its limits, and its needs. It's hard to say if you ever really thought about yourself being a living thing inside a fleshy vessel before, but as the months and weeks pass, it's pretty much all you can think of.

Is a twinge in a muscle a symptom of something or just a reflex? Is the insatiable hunger a result of steroids or a sign of something worse? Will your vision return?

Is any of this normal? Will it ever get better?

"Right."

Mum stands at the bottom of the stairs and bellows.

"That's dinner ready!"

You hear the shuffle of feet from desks upstairs. They probably stand in their temporary offices, stretching the day hunched at the desk off their shoulders. Yawn and stretch, shuffle to the door. Rub the screen from their eyes. Rub their bellies.

Do they think about every movement as they open the door and walk down the stairs into the kitchen, or is it automatic for them? Are their bodies in one-way conversations with their minds?

The front door goes. Your brother's family charge in from the guest house at the end of the garden. His two little boys, one young enough to cling to his mum's hip still, the other older and stamping to the kitchen roaring like a dinosaur.

"Take your shoes off!"

His Mum calls from the front door, the youngest babbling from her hip.

The Dino child stomps back and strips the Velcro from his feet, then continues to roar through the house.

Family is someone to call you brother, uncle, or son. Someone to drink beer with, kick a rugby ball or grab your hand when the rapid water of life starts to pull you under. But most of all, family means noise to you.

The buzz from the kitchen draws everybody in like a magnet. Mum orchestrates them around the table- you hear her gather plates, rattle cutlery together and scrape chairs into new positions. Wine is poured, beer cans burst open, and juice fills the kids.

The house now erupts with life. From the silent living room, it calls you in, beckoning you to come.

Outside, a storm gathers in dark skies and the wind continues to roar. Rain hammers on the street, blotting out any glimpse of daylight to a premature night.

But none of that exists here. As you stand alone in the living room, you feel the warmth of the family pull you in.

Move your body towards the door, your sock finds the damp patch in the rug. It soaks through and leaves a faint damp imprint with every step you take.

Pause outside the living room door, your hand gripping onto the frame. Behind you is the memory of the news and a series of tragedies that have locked the world away from one another. Your hand peels from the edge of the door and you push on.

From the end of the corridor, your blurred vision can hardly make out who's moving in the soft warm light of the kitchen. But you aren't led by sight anymore.

You are drawn in by the prospect of mum's cooking, the warm invitation to the taste of your childhood. The smell of the past mingles with the voices of the present, new generations of family learning the value of the dinner table.

Voices spill from the kitchen and ricochet down the hallway. Mum and Dad bicker over who forgot to put white wine on the online shop. Your brother cuts in saying he's got a bottle in the fridge back at theirs. A dinosaur roars and bangs his knife and fork on the table, setting his brother off with a hearty child's laugh.

The noises swirl around you, the walls of the hall closing and expanding with each breath.

Bang goes the cutlery. Roar goes the dinosaur.

The walls expand and contract.

The door opens. An arm wraps around you, grips you and brings the world to right.

"You're okay."

Mum stands there, a smile on her face that stops the walls from spinning.

"Let's get you to the table."
"Mum..."

Your arm reaches out and finds her shoulder.
She turns, a slight wrinkle of worry falling across her brow. She looks at you, asking if everything is alright with a single expression.
Standing in your wet sock, you think about the lifetime of footprints that led you here. Through hospital wards and surgery theatres- the hallways of shitty jobs, kitchens and university, a time that almost crushed you with loneliness.
That shaky trail was you finding your feet, a journey that started so long ago in this very house, and one you demand has not yet finished.
Because for every time you stood on your own two feet- from the very beginning, baby faced and drooling through to right now - there has always been someone there for you.

"What's up love?"

Pull her towards you, your arms loose around her neck.

"Thanks."

Her arms wrap around you, squeezing you harder than anyone else could ever manage - just like the very first time you walked right into her arms.

PROCRASTINATION

*I'm writing a poem because I'm procrastinating and
bored, I tried thinking of something more profound, but
it takes more than a phone to turn inspiration around.
How does that sound? It's not exactly profound, more
like a clown in a shed typing on a phone.*

*I'll give it this, it's a relaxing form of procrastinating and
it's my time to waste and I'll waste it at my own pace.
You can pass time in haste but that would defeat the
purpose, and that's the last thing I'd want.*

*Here's the thing though, what is the purpose of this,
maybe I should know. I could try to do a show or release
a book. If you could lend me the energy that took then
can you spare a motivational change please?*

*I'm not exactly seizing the day in a way to resolve the
issue but the issue is mine and I think it requires
thought and time. You see how quick you return to the*

procrastinating pit? It's at breakneck pace, so fast the
space around my inactivity rips and collapses in a sonic
boom. You'll hear it soon if you're patient, hang on it
might have got distracted or tired and quit. You really
can't rely on sound precipitation coming from activity
based on procrastination.

The first few weeks and months were filled with milestones and nervous tension. The whole family waiting with bated breath for the results of the first scans after the surgery.

Then it was all about getting up and out of bed and moving around. A wiggle of a toe or a clenched fist became huge moments to be celebrated. The whole thing felt like climbing a mountain and everybody cheered you on as you edged towards the top.

There was always something new around the corner and your focus was only on the ridge just up ahead. There's no need to think about what was further up the mountain, you just need to get past this next hurdle before you move onto the next. The weight of expectation disappeared and all everybody cared about was you getting better. That hasn't changed, but over the months, the milestones got few and far between.

You're up and about now, making your own cups of tea and going to the toilet without the embarrassing ritual. You're not ready to get back into normal life just yet but you're past the struggle of basic mobility. That leaves you stuck somewhere in the middle, drowning in time to kill, the long months punctuated by the odd chemo sessions.

It's half eleven in the morning and you've nothing to show for it so far. You've just been kicking around in the shed, willing an idea into your head but it doesn't come. You're hoping for something profound to capture the unique nature of your situation, to pour the whirlwind of emotions onto the page and create something that no one can forget.

There must be some way to immortalise this experience in a few simple lines, but in the end, nothing comes. You're just looking for something to do until lunch, so you start hammering words into your phone to see where they go.

True, it's no masterpiece but it's better than sitting around watching TV. For the first time in weeks, you feel like you've accomplished the impossible- but in some sense, you're wishing the time away so you can get back to normality.

It's only recently that events have changed the way you see things. Every second, even the ones you spend procrastinating are worth savouring.

So, you sit in your shed, typing away into your phone in the hope that you'll latch onto a good idea and it'll transport you somewhere.

It gives you respite for half an hour and that sense of movement returns. The boredom disappears and you start chugging along at the same pace as the world instead of being stuck motionless in your shed, waiting for something to happen.

What that something is, you're still not sure, and that's why your momentum doesn't last long. You don't have anything to drive for so it's easy to fall back into the pit.

The chemo is draining everything out of you. The nausea and aching make every movement heavy, but you feel so empty that you could be transparent.

The gaps between each round are an opportunity to get moving but it feels like you barely get back on your feet before it's time to start again. An endless Groundhog Day loop of almost doing something. It's like taking a huge run-up and then, just before you jump, you hit an invisible wall and slowly drag yourself back to the start line.

Procrastination is the best you can manage right now, and you're trying your hardest to make sure that its at least worthwhile time wasted. You've already burnt so much time in the past wishing things were different, but now you feel compelled to make it so.

Before any of this, you let the hard times flatten you and squeeze you dry like a toothpaste tube. How many days did you spend alone in the dark, willing your life away when you should have been out there, taking in every second?

Every time you put on a false smile and gave another rehearsed 'it's all fine 'you missed an opportunity to put yourself back together and start living. You can't blame yourself, though.

At the time, it felt like you were locked into that moment and things would never move on. You felt so guilty about the horrible feelings inside because you felt like you had no right to them.

The thing is, there's never any logic to it. There's not a thing that makes you feel that way, you just do. You weren't prepared to deal with the constant left turns of life and you felt wrong for being unhappy, so you locked it inside and let it fester.

But now, you're finally letting yourself be unhappy and that's always a good thing. The guilt has gone because, when you've got a hole in your head, nobody can accuse you of overplaying the situation and complaining about nothing.

Let the shit days be shit and trying to get something out of the good days. But that doesn't stop you from wishing you could go back and change things. If you had this mentality before then life could have been different.

The period of time that disappeared into shit jobs, cans of lager and self-loathing is lost. Now that time seems so precious, you wish you hadn't wasted it.

After a few moments of typing, you stop dead. You've run out of any ideas to jot down. The blinking cursor mocks you as you desperately reach around in your head for something else to put on the page- Something, anything to keep the flow going, even if it isn't great. Because, you know, when the flow stops, you're dragged at breakneck speeds right back into inactivity.

The idea never comes and you find yourself, once again, sitting in a shed, killing time. Sigh, stand and march out into the garden.

The early Spring sun brings flashes of warmth to the chilly air, which hasn't quite caught up yet. It sparkles in the remnants of the morning dew and makes the lawn look delicate.

The quiet is crushing. Everybody goes about their day, so much to do, rushing and trying desperately to find the time for everything.

You, on the other hand, stand in the garden, staring into the sky and desperately hope that you'll stumble on something to do to fill the rest of the afternoon.

Instead, you end up daydreaming about the most mundane things. Usually, when people dream of being somewhere else, they're thinking of something exciting. People want to revisit their favourite holidays or cherished childhood memories.

But all you want is to be back in one of the boring jobs you hated so much at the time. The monotony of waiting tables or sitting in an office, calling up strangers or serving drinks seems so comforting right now.

Sure, it wasn't worthwhile but at least it had some kind of end goal. The days and weeks were broken down into simple chunks. An eight-hour shift then head home, another day ticked off.

These days, it all merges into one. Get up when you feel like it, eat something, watch TV, maybe try to write for a bit, stand in the garden, kick yourself for procrastinating, have lunch, repeat.

Speaking of, it's time for lunch, so you start making a move towards the house. The last round of chemo still lays heavy as you hobble over the grass, feeling the cold dew soak through your shoes. The tightness in your chest becomes more strained as you drag yourself across the garden.

When you make it into the kitchen, lean against the side for a moment to catch your breath. Everything you do takes a frustrating amount of effort and just getting around leaves you precious little energy for anything else.

Decide on a sandwich for lunch and set about the long, laborious process of putting it together. Something that is normally muscle memory now requires intense concentration.

Taking the bread out is usually the easiest part, but the little plastic tab thing is tricky to get off with shaky fingers and blurred vision in one eye. Spend a few minutes wrestling with it, twisting it this way and that. Every time you pull at it feels like you're making it tighter. You're going red in the face as you give up on the careful approach and just start randomly yanking at it. Eventually, it rips open and you throw the bag down on the side and try to calm down.

Now the hard part, buttering the bread. The careful, precise movements take every ounce of mental energy that you have left. Don't press too hard, you don't want to rip the bread, just glide gently over the top and take your time with it. You manage the first slice with relative ease.

On the second, overconfidence gets the better of you and a big clump of butter grabs hold of the bread, tearing it open. Frustration rises in your chest and you feel a strong urge to chuck the whole thing in the bin. But even that seems like too much hard work, and you don't have the drive to be angry right now. You've buttered one and a half slices, that's good enough. Throw in some ham and be done with it.

Even getting the crisps open is an effort but, eventually, you manage to sit down for some lunch. You look at the clock and laugh- if there was a record for the longest time to make a ham sandwich, you'd take it.

As you stare out of the window to the empty street, you feel like you're in an old prison movie. One of those ones where they sit around in the exercise yard, talking about all the things they're going to do when they finally get out of this place. There are always the young kids that have the crazy plans to get rich and travel the world.

The old guys just laugh at them, their plans are much simpler. They just want a quiet life with good people around them and enough money in the bank to get by.

In some ways, you're like the old guys now, picturing how simple life should be. But you're also like the young guys with their big aspirations. You want something exciting out of life and you were on the way to finding it before you got locked up in this prison of medically induced apathy.

It feels like you're one of the ambitious young guys trapped in the body of the old timer that can't really remember what it's like to be on the outside.

A full belly slows the day to a halt and from there it's so easy to just reach for the TV remote. It's that afternoon dead zone when all the morning programs have finished but the teatime quizzes haven't started yet. You flick through a few detective shows but the cheesy lines and over-the-top haircuts are too much to bear.

Instead, you manage twenty minutes watching a retired post office worker and his wife, a dog groomer, start a new life on the Costa Del Sol. You're only half watching because you want to see how they can drag this out into an hour-long program but really, you're not even taking it in. The peaceful shots of sunny beaches and stray cats on hot cobbled streets are mildly comforting, even though there isn't much substance. A nice junk food snack for your brain after a taxing morning of doing not much at all.

The credits roll and the voiceover woman announces yet another episode. If you watch two in a row, you're locked in and that's the rest of the day gone, so you start flicking again.

An old episode of Millionaire is on. Shouting the occasional answer at the TV at least feels like achieving something. If you wanted, you could say this is a way to keep your brain active. So, you sit for a while, half listening to the questions and blurting out answers. You get a couple right and feel mildly proud of yourself.

Convince yourself that this is a good use of your day, that an afternoon with Chris Tarrant is better than staring for hours at a blank page. It doesn't take long before you feel that niggling sense of time dripping away.

Switch it up again, find something more interesting. Maybe a documentary is on somewhere and you could learn something, nobody can say that's a waste of time. Search desperately through the endless stream of light entertainment and sitcom repeats but find nothing.

Eventually, you get past the normal stuff and into the shopping channels. As you keep scrolling, the rest of the programs disappear and you're left with a wall of 'teleshopping'.

Hit the off button. There's no justifying it now, you're well and truly wasting time. When the glaring picture cuts, you're faced with a reflection of yourself in the black screen. You feel the guilt wash over you as you stare at the person in the TV, a limp and frail body.

Push yourself upright and check the time. It's getting on for five already and apart from a ham sandwich and half a poem, you haven't achieved much of anything today. Go back to the kitchen and clean up the fallout from lunch. When you're done, it's tempting to put the TV back on. You know that there's a good few hours of quiz shows and then The Simpsons is on. You could lean into the procrastination but decide against it.

Instead, you head back outside to the shed. The nice afternoon sun is dipping now. The trees around the garden cast a long shadow as the blood orange ball cuts between them. The hairs on your arms stand up as you shuffle back over to the clinking patio slabs down to the shed. Once inside, you grab your jumper and throw it on, huddling into yourself and trying to get comfortable.

Take out your phone and start reading back over the few lines that you wrote this morning. When you started it, you were just killing time. But reading it now, you can see the potential, a fragment in the words that wants to say the same thing you do.

You've spent the last few years documenting your life in short bursts. It's been a constant background feature of your life, but you never really thought about what you were doing it for. What was its purpose? Does it need one?

Maybe, maybe not. For now, it's just a way to pass the time and organise your own head. It still has value, even if it's just something that you wrote in the shed one afternoon because you couldn't bear to watch another minute of daytime TV.

Is it wasted time if it was relaxing and you enjoyed it while you were doing it? Try not to think too much about it, just carry on and see what happens.

Still, the idea of giving it some purpose, sending it out into the world does appeal to you. It's terrifying, in a way, but also exciting. Instead of killing time you could be using it to make something beautiful. Either way, you should finish this poem.

The rest of it comes easily and starts to shape into the thing you imagined it to be. In the past, whenever you typed rushed lines into your phone at the back of a bus or when you couldn't sleep, it felt like releasing a balloon into the wind. You watched it float off and if you looked hard enough, you could see it as a dot in the sky.

But writing now feels like carving into a concrete block. Every word is carefully considered and placed because you have a feeling that they'll be on display for a long time to come.

They're no longer a fleeting idea born from empty time, they're a solid fixture that has been constructed with care.

Spend the next few hours buried in your phone as the world moves on outside your shed. You don't notice the sun make its final descent beyond the horizon as the moon creeps in and casts a crystal white reflection on your little window. The cold air whistling through the gaps in the wood doesn't bother you.

You don't even look up when the wind rushes through and rattles the door.

You only notice how long it's been when you hear the house come to life. Make your final adjustments and put the phone down. As you look out of the window, you see the kitchen lights come on. Mum and dad are milling around, probably deciding what to have for tea. You realise then just how hungry you are.

Lights flick on throughout the house as they go about their normal routine. You sit there and watch for a few minutes. Eventually, the back door opens and dad walks down the garden on his way to say hello and ask how your day has been.

Tell him that you didn't get a whole lot done really. Just a bit of procrastinating, but it was time well wasted.

RUM DRINKS AND PERFECT TANS

The worst thing about cancer is it's cowardly and indirect. Because it's really attacking my friends and family that have to wait and see how it ends. I know it ends in victory, it's the patch of future I can clearly see like a squeegee swipe on a dirty window, the soap is parted to show us laughing on for eternity.

I can also see challenges for each and all but few to this degree and with all the stocked-up luck the daily ought to become a luxury.

Non-stop luck for me and us is just on the horizon so let's keep our eyes on the skyline. The sun is coming up and we will become unstuck from this coral reef, we'll avoid the grief, and the moral of the story will be not even the turbulent fate at sea can capsize you and me in our mahogany family vessel.

We just need to wrestle with the rigging until we hit our top velocity and go clipping over the waves on our voyage to fonder days. That's the treasure we're going to plunder, I found the X hidden under a boulder, with us, we can shoulder the weight undoubtedly. It might be a tight fit, but we can squeeze under and take our plunder

back on the ship and have a victory sip of G&T on deck,
and let people wonder how the heck did they get those
rum drinks, perfect tans and get rich so quick?

"We'll have to take the long route."

Your brother fingers the map on his phone, arms resting on the steering wheel.

A nurse opens the door in the space next to you, clicks the car locked and walks to the entrance. Outside, she stops and puts on a mask. Your head turns to the back.

The kids are quietly sleeping away. Turn in your seat and watch gentle baby breaths fill their lungs, the odd sigh pushed from their tiny mouth's. The radio plays almost silently, the inane talk from the presenters filling the space inside the car.

Your brother taps away at the screen, shutting one eye as he maps a route home. He falls back in the seat and sighs. The traffic home from the hospital is tricky around this time.

The engine hums to life and fans cool air across your face. Outside the sky is bright but grey, a hazy light settling across the car park. It's not warm and it's not cold, the weather undecided whether it's spring or winter.

You creep through the maze of cars, stopping every so often to let someone cross the road.

Ignoring the odd nurse or doctor, you spend the short drive watching small groups navigate through the slow traffic. They walk guided by the hand or arm of a loved one. Others move with more purpose, their careful steps filled with a cautious optimism. You can see it in the way they take in their surroundings.

You roll to a stop at the give way, waiting for the car in front to join the mess of traffic around the hospital. A man around your age steps out of a car beside you. His wife gets out the other side. Their faces are pale, rings under their eyes thick with worry. They must be new to all this.

He opens the door, leans in and gently lifts a young girl from the seat. The woman stares at the floor as her daughter's head droops over his shoulder, asleep.

You pray that they aren't here for her, that they are maybe visiting a loved one or something. Anything that isn't the reason everyone else comes here.

But no amount of reason or prayers helps to ease the reality of this place. Cancer is a dark cloud, uncaring to anything but its own survival and happy to strike anyone in its way.

For most of your life, it was something that happened to other people. A tragedy, but a fact of existence that could be managed by not thinking about it. Why?

Because when it happens to you, it happens to everyone else you know too.

You turn into the traffic and stop almost immediately at a red light. Elbow on the window, press your hand against your head, fingers squeezing at your throbbing temples.

You're crashing, a wild downturn fuelled by the bitter tasting steroids coursing through your system. The cool air blowing from the car strips you dry, tongue scraping the inside of your mouth. You swallow a hard lump of air and let your head roll on the headrest.

"You ok?"

One hand on the wheel and an eye on the road, your brother hands you a small lunchbox.

"There's a drink and stuff in there."

The light flicks to green and the car rolls across the junction, hitting another red light in a matter of seconds. You feel the roll of tires on tarmac surround you. Tearing the

Velcro strip, you open the bottle and take huge gulps. You gasp with the half empty bottle crushed in your hand.

It's not good, but it's better than before. The world passing by the car seems to slow down again, righting the spinning sensation that drowned you in the sound of traffic.

"Thanks."

You heave through a breathless voice.

"The steroids are usually fine but today…"

You gag in the quiet of the car and topple back in your seat.

"You want me to stop somewhere?"

Shake your head and shut your eyes, the gentle road rocking you from side to side. The faint hum of the car fades into the dark of your eyes. All three of you quietly nap through the traffic, your brother gently drumming his fingers on the wheel.

For that moment the car is a soft vessel on a calm ocean. As the world grinds on through the stop start of traffic, the three of you lock yourself inside the gentle thoughts of a tired mind. Another red light, the car lurches to a halt.

The silence cracks in two, startling everyone from their slumber.

"Jesus."

He calls out from next to you, leaning forward to scan the sky above the car.

Your brittle eyes dart from side to side and settle on a spray of bird shit down the windshield. A squirt of fluid dribbles over the white streak, the wipers smearing it from side to side and leaving a fine mist of shit across the screen.

"I hate seagulls."

He's trying to look annoyed, glaring at the sky as if finding the culprit will change anything.

He turns to you, shaking his head. The minute your eyes meet, a smile creeps across your face for the first time today.

A chesty laugh bursts through the car, startling the kids in the back fully awake. The light turns green, and you move slowly through the junction.

"Did you see the size of that thing?"

He takes another glimpse at the sky. A car horn blares up ahead of you.

"Dad."

A tiny voice calls out, his hand rubbing the sleep from his eye. He looks at him through the rear-view.

"Sorry buddy, did we wake you up?"

You turn in your seat and flash a big grin at the little man in the back. The baby starts to babble a little, his legs kicking from the chair.

"Have you seen this?"

He laughs and points at the windshield.

"Some naughty bird has done a big poo on the car."

He wraps his hand over his mouth and giggles. Your brother shakes his head as the traffic breaks and he accelerates through the busy street, squinting every so often through the misted screen.

The sun begins to break through the clouds, flashing golden Spring rays across the bonnet and windshield. You can see every flake of slowly crusting poo through the glass. Your head rolls towards your brother.

"Hey, when was the last time you went through a carwash?"
"I actually don't know."

He scratches his head and looks in the rear-view.

"Don't know if the boys have ever been through one."
"What do we think guys?"

You spin around in your seat, smile and nod your head.

"Should your dad take us through the carwash?"

He doesn't know what a carwash is, but he cheers and slaps his chubby toddler hands together anyway. The baby starts to gurgle a little happy sound.

"Yeah, alright then."

He flicks the indicator and changes lane.

"I think there's one down the way here."

In a couple of minutes, the car wheels through a business park and turns into the carwash. A small buff man in a hi-vis struts across the forecourt with a rag thrown over his shoulder. He takes a ratty mask from out of his pocket and layers it across his thick beard. The window sighs as it opens.

"No interior, just outside, ok?"

He starts to motion the car onto the tracks.

"Polish also?"
"Just a clean please mate."

He reaches in his wallet, sliding a ten-pound note in the man's thick hands.

The car creeps along, wheels locking into the metal tracks. A red light above the entrance shines through the shit on the windscreen, momentarily stinging your good eye. He kills the engine.

Two younger guys get up from the plastic school chairs at the side with buckets in their hands. They start to wipe down bits of the car with rags, throwing suds across the windshield and bonnet.

The seatbelt unclips beside you and he turns to the kids in the back.

"Everyone good back there?"

He reaches across and jostles the eldest's foot.

"Dad, where are we?"

He watches the cloth swipe back on forth on his window.

"This is the carwash bud."

He smiles, turns back and nudges you.

"Remember when dad would take us through these as a kid?"

255

You nod along with a deep smile on your face. You think you remember, like little flashes of being in the backseat on a booster with your two brothers beside you. But the harder you think, the less you recall.

There was fighting and screaming over leg space, you know that much. Snacks passed from the front were used to pacify arguments, leaving crumbs and chocolate in your lap.

There were dark nights and long drives home from your grandparents, flashes of orange streetlights guiding you. But try as you might, you can't remember the carwash at all.

The light above you flashes green and you jerk forward on the conveyor belt. The world outside the window goes dark, the sound of rushing water and the whir of moving parts surrounding the vehicle.

The tunnel drags you in to the darkness. A small glimmer of light appears at the end, but otherwise there is only roaring and black. Neon blues erupt through the windows, illuminating a wall of water which cascades down from the ceiling. The light flashes, turning the soap suds into glaring shades of purple, green and orange.

A mechanic whipping starts to ripple along metal, dragging closer to you. The little straps of brushes slap against the screen, peel and fly off in a hypnotic rhythm.

You both turn to watch the boys' reaction to the wonderland outside. They are fixed in their seats, save for the lone hand pressing back against the glass, hoping to feel a glimmer of the strange world outside.

"Wow!"

He mouths out the word.

"Dad look!"

A finger juts towards the sunroof as the tentacles graze against the glass and crawl to the rear.

A squeak of glee comes from the baby seat. You answer -

"That's right buddy, can you see all the pretty colours?"

He rocks back and forth, babbling and dribbling through the light show. Roll back in your seat and shut your one good eye.

A fine mist settles and drips down the car and blue flashes of light shine over the windscreen. In the short bursts of colour, you try focus your strained vision on the rush of parts.

Your eyes start to roll with the flickering of the lights. You strain them both open which does little to cease the turns inside your mind. If you could, you'd open the window and let a wave of cool air crash across your fragile pale skin. Instead, you sit there, churning in the quiet of the car.

Momentary bouts of nausea. That's how the doctor described it.

You'd describe it more like, reality catching up with you.

Shut your eyes and ignore the plea from your body for room to vomit. Through your eyelids, you feel the lights flash from green to red.

Control your breathing and relax your shoulders. There's some comfort in being dragged through the colours this way. Static yet still moving. If you didn't need to throw up, you'd probably chuckle at the metaphorical ride you're on.

Sure, there are moments where it can seem overwhelming, but you know it will be worth it when you come out the other side. It's become a bit of a mantra for you- this can only get better.

Strips of fans start to blow air across the car, dragging the stray suds and droplets of water off the body. He starts the engine as the tunnel ends and the golden light outside shines over the beaming faces in the car.

"Wow"

A tiny voice calls from the back.

"Dad, can we go again?"
"I think we're clean enough."

He waves at the man with the beard, easing through the narrow exit and back into the road.

Your pocket buzzes. Navigate fingers into the tight jeans, wrestling in the seat to work your phone out. Through your good eye, you read the text.

"It's mum. Looks like it's just us for dinner tonight."
"Huh"

He stops at another red light, teeth nipping at the fingernails on one hand.

"Anything you fancy?"
"I'm easy."

Slot the phone between your legs.

"Whatever it is though, I need a lot of it."
"Alright."

He smiles and brings the car through the junction.

"I've got us covered there."

Hitting green at the next set of lights, he takes a hard right and revs through a narrow country lane. Soon the bustle of the streets gives way to rolling hills filled with cows, sheep and horses.

As the afternoon sun starts to beam through the dispersing clouds, flashes of blue cloak the horizon of green pastures. The road winds between valleys and rivers, rising and dipping to meet the bend of the earth.

There's a sense in you that somewhere, you've seen this road before, the bends and twists alive in your head somewhere. Maybe this is the exact drive dad would do all those years ago, your memory a remnant of that blissful period of life.

The car swerves along the road, dipping before rising to overlook the sea. The sun carves across white beaches, the dark silhouette of a pier stretching out into the glimmer of light on the water. Beyond that, the ocean roars.

"Anyone fancy a dip in the sea?"

It's impossible not to smile when the childish shouts and kicks rattle the backseat.

Your brother turns to you and points along the road.

"Thought we could get a chippy before we headed home."

The day is getting better, a proper fish supper sounds -

"Perfect."

Outside the cosy confines of the road, the afternoon sun starts to sink in the sky, turning the water on the horizon deep shades of red and orange. You find a picnic bench overlooking the pier and sit there with one hand rocking the buggy.

Despite how sunny it's turned, you all keep your coats on and shoulders hunched. A ring of seagulls flies above you, your brother taking a moment between chips to glare at them. His shoulders hunch over the food as he forks another bit of fish into his mouth.

"Are you looking to scrap a seagull?"

You smile at him and shove a handful of chips in.
"If it comes for my supper, I might do."

A sharp gust of wind blows over the table, sending shivers down your neck. Your arms squeeze against the cold, teeth clenched tight together.

"We can eat these in the car if you want?"
"I'm good."

You sit up straight, body feeling stronger with the warmth in your stomach. You could do another portion, easily.
Beneath the occasional call from the seagulls, the ocean gathers crashing waves against the sand.
There's a gurgle from inside the pram. A plastic dinosaur flies out and rattles on the ground. You bend over, dust off the body and give it back to him.
Your brother shakes his head and smiles. The dinosaur snaps against the floor, followed by a frenzy of laughter.

"It's a losing battle, trust me."

He rolls his eyes and goes in for a few more chips.
One by one, you all finish your food. The seagulls move closer towards the bench in the hope of a scrap.

"Dad?"

Tiny greased up fingers jut across the bench.

"What's that?"

Your brother cranes his neck, a glowing smile across his face.

"Come on, I'll show you."

He takes his son by the hand and hops to his feet. You lean into the pram, pulling a silly face and grunting.

Hand in hand, the little one toddles his legs as fast as he can, light up shoes flashing against the dark grey paving stones.

"Right, go around the other side and put your head through that hole."

Your brother swings around and shouts back to the bench.

"You want to get a picture together?"

They both stand looking at a crude cartoon on a large piece of wood, the head of both figures cut out revealing the red brick behind it.

It takes a second to put your body upright, the cold locks your knees and hips in the sitting position. Smile and walk the pram around the bench, parking it beside your brother.

"Come on uncle."

He peers from around the wood with his hand out, bouncing from one leg to the other.

"I'm coming."

You shuffle your stiff body and take his hand.

"Right, so just put your head through that hole there."

He stops and looks a touch lost.

"Just like this see."

Bend and slot your face through the gap in the wood. Your brother stands on the other side with a huge grin on his face.

"Alright you two."

He holds his phone up.

"Smile!"

A small beam of light flashes against the luminous orange sky. Your eyes sting. He takes another. The flash ripples through your vision again, blinding you for a split second.

He examines the picture and bursts out with the same chesty giggle you've known for your whole life. Little footsteps scatter behind you, pure excitement in the childish gallops across the pavement.

Your brother crouches down to show him the picture. They tilt their head back and begin to laugh together, like father like son.

"Uncle look!"

He points at the photo and shouts.

In it, you stand on a sunny beach, Hawaiian shirt unbuttoned to reveal a perfectly sculpted chest and a cocktail in hand. One leg is cocked up and resting on an open treasure chest- jewels, gold and pearls spilling out of pockets. A baby seal with a small child's head beams a silly grin from the side.

"Alright boys"

He slaps his hands together and starts to push the pram.

"Let's get back to the car."

Bellies full of chips and the smell of salt water deep in your mind, it's hard to get rid of the smile on your face. Stop and turn back to the vacant picture behind you, imagining the feel of sun on skin and an ice-cold cocktail in hand.

It can all still be yours. There's not a shadow of doubt about it. The sun, the drinks and the treasure; it's all for the taking.

Turn and follow the three figures up ahead. Your brother slows down, turns and waves to you. You wave back.

You've never been more certain of finding treasure in your life.

SECRET

There was a mystery that for years perplexed me. The more adult life became clear, I couldn't see how you could do it and be genuinely happy with all that responsibility and a severe fantasy deficiency. It became a real issue, I was sure I wouldn't find a way through, but then I came to a conclusion that was undeniably true, and I'm going to tell it to you. Let me know if you agree or if this is just me.

You can literally have cake for dinner if you like. Now for the sake of your health you probably won't but I implore that you do! And wash it down with a Coke.

Familiarity is a paradox. It's comforting yet restrictive at the same time. Being in your childhood home, every room filled with memories, instantly brings you back to a simpler time. Every small detail of the house is a reminder of being young, before the responsibility started to creep in.

You're quick to fall back into old habits. You take the same seat on the sofa, use the same mug for your tea.

Being surrounded by family gives you a safety net, this existence a shield against the looming responsibilities that lies on the other side of the ordeal. When you eventually step forth from your nostalgic cocoon, will you be ready?

Dad comes through to the living room while you're watching TV. Everybody else is out for the day so it's just the two of you. He parks next to you on the sofa and asks if there's anything better on. Doubtful, but at least something different. Chuck him the remote and he starts flicking through the channels. Nobody watches TV on a Saturday afternoon, so it's all just repeats of programmes you never wanted to watch the first time around.

The boredom is setting in now. This is where the paradox comes into play. The familiarity might be comforting, but it's so draining at the same time. The days roll into one as you look for ways to kill time. The waves of treatment ebb and flow. You hold on to the time in between when you have the energy to do things but before you know it, the cycle begins again.

With time, the familiarity becomes so much less comforting because you're not a kid anymore. The mundane days matter more now because there's no fantasy to counteract them.

Is that what growing into an adult is? Letting go of the dreams and fantasies and settling into the mountain of responsibilities. Maybe you just need to lean into the things you've been shying away from, push your thumb into the bruise and relish in the ache a little bit. Maybe that's the secret.

You wonder how they all do it. Everybody around you seems to have embraced adulthood and all it brings with open arms. Dad is buried under the crushing weight of responsibility but he doesn't let it phase him. He gets up and goes to work and he shoulders that burden without complaining. That's the way it's always been. In every situation he's always the pragmatic one, never wasting time on the 'why 'or 'how', just looking for a solution.

You suppose it works for him because he knows what he's doing. He has everything worked out, every fine detail planned, nothing is left to chance. It's easy for him to keep ticking along, day by day, without letting responsibility crush him. His life is very tangible while yours exists in a more abstract way.

It's not fine-tuned cogs whirring away that keep you moving forward each day, it's the fantasies and bold ideas. It's the thought of diving headfirst off a cliff and hoping that you survive that keeps you going.

You look over to him, straight-faced, watching an old episode of Only Fools and Horses. There's not even a slight twitch when the punchlines roll in. The TV lets out a laugh but he just watches on. He could just as easily be watching a tragedy unfold on the news, there's no way to tell the difference.

You look closer but his face gives nothing away. There's not a hint of an explanation, you're still struggling to work out what his secret is. How does he have everything so painstakingly put together without a hint of the unexpected?

You've always wondered this- it's often why you feel like you're different. The rest of the family seem to slot things in place so easily. They marched on into adulthood and left any notions of fantasy behind in their childhood while you still feel stuck somewhere in between.

The responsibilities of adulthood pile on but you still don't feel like you've got all the answers worked out. You're certainly not ready to let go of those notions of fantasy either. Maybe you'll never find the secret and work out how to fit everything together.

Let out a yawn and stretch your back- the hours of sinking into the sofa have tied it in knots. Dad looks over as you try to loosen it up.

"How are you feeling?"

Tell him you're fine. He didn't want to ask in the first place. Not because he doesn't care, but because it hurts. He knows the real answer isn't good and he doesn't want to hear it. Who would?

"Tea?"
"Thanks."

He gets up and heads to the kitchen. You watch him scan through the cupboards, fingers stretched out as he racks his brain. He's seen it done plenty of times, but he can't remember the last time he did it himself. Mum's probably reorganised the kitchen since the last time he made tea and that's thrown him. You laugh as you watch him struggle. It's a rare sight to see him lost.

"Cupboard over the sink."

He nods and grabs two mugs. He flicks the kettle on and starts scanning again. There's something satisfying about watching him figure it out. It's like seeing a magician mess up his trick. The curtain falls and the illusion is broken. It's all just sleight of hand and clever misdirection, not some unbreakable secret.

Eventually, he finds the teabags and manages to make a passable cup of tea. You thank him as he sets it down next to you and sinks into the sofa again.

Sitting in silence, sipping at a mug of tea is just fine. You're glad that everybody's stopped trying so hard now. In the beginning, everybody was trying so hard to say the right thing and it was suffocating. But over time, everybody settled into the routine, and it became part of the normal day-to-day- in some ways the old dynamic returned. That kind of familiarity is comforting.

Dad struggled after your diagnosis. He instantly buried himself in practicality and solutions, which you needed, but it didn't hide the fear. The curtain had been pulled back and there he was, faced with this thing he couldn't control. This didn't happen because he did things wrong, and it couldn't have been prevented if he did things differently. It just happened and no amount of planning or sensible decisions could have stopped it.

It's almost five, you only had a sandwich for lunch so you're getting hungry. You could get up for a snack but you feel locked in. The will to move is there but it's small and the TV wins, so you just ignore the niggling in your stomach. It'll fade away soon anyway.

Dad shuffles in his chair and glances over to the kitchen. You don't remember him having any lunch at all, he was busy doing something for work. He must be starving, but he decides against getting up too and goes back to the TV.

You both glaze over and let the screen play on in the background. All the stress starts to fall away and you float in the feeling for a while. There's no need for long conversations and reassuring sentiments to make you feel better. People often mistake the rigidity for a lack of feeling but he doesn't need to tell you he cares- you see it in what he does. He's a man of action, not words, and sitting here watching TV in silence is his way of being there for you. After all the panic, it's refreshing to just sit for a while.

You watch the figures on the TV move around, but the sound disappears into nothing. Let your head empty for a while, not thinking about responsibilities or plans. Your eyelids start drooping and each blink lasts a little longer.

Your limbs go heavy and you begin losing control over your body as you gently drift off. In the final moments before you fall asleep you feel like a child again. You enjoy the feeling of knowing that dad is shouldering the responsibilities and you just need to float through your days, not worrying about anything.

But the feeling doesn't last long. You're thrown back into the present when the phone goes. The shrill screeching cuts through the peaceful bubble in front of the TV and startles you both.

Rub your claggy eyes and sit up. Dad sighs and heaves himself from the chair. As you watch him go over to answer the phone, you suddenly become aware of how hungry you are. The slight niggling has grown into a dense ball. The acidic sting pulls your stomach inwards and crawls up your throat. You check the time, it's almost seven.

It looks like dad is locked into a serious conversation. His brow is furrowed, leaning forward with one hand planted on the kitchen counter. With each nod, the lines on his face tighten and his shoulders creep towards his ears. It looks like he's winding up, ready to let loose, but he never does. He just absorbs the stress and it disappears somewhere. After a few curt instructions and a very formal goodbye, he puts the phone down and heads upstairs.

You look over at the TV and suddenly, the sight of it frustrates you. Switch it off and get out of your chair, you need some food.

Walk into the kitchen and stop for a second, deciding where to look first. You're in one of those moods where you're hungry for everything but you can't put your finger on exactly what you want.

Open the fridge and scan up and down the shelves. A bit of ham, but you already had that in a sandwich for lunch. There are some eggs but you can't be bothered with the hassle of cooking them. A bit of leftover cake from one of the boy's birthdays, but that's hardly a meal. What would dad say if he came down to find you halfway through a slice of cake?

There's not much else in the fridge. The cupboards are packed full of things that don't quite hit the spot. In the end, you grab a packet of crisps to plug the gap while you decide.

Dad comes down, looking exhausted. He hardly lifts his feet as he comes down the stairs, hanging his head a bit. You can see the tension in his bunched-up shoulders and stiff neck. He walks into the kitchen and, on seeing you, straightens up. The unconvincing smile comes across his face instantly, like he feels guilty for being stressed. He's trying hard but the mask slipped for a split second and you saw just how tired he was.

He grabs a glass of water and stares into the garden for a few moments before turning to you.

"Shall we go for a walk, get out of the house for a bit?"

Nobody bothered too much about your exercise routine before, but now everybody seems adamant that you have regular walks to stay fit and healthy. You complain, but you're glad of the chance to get outside for a while. The treatment and the boredom are sapping your energy and you need to get moving to give yourself a boost.

It's a nice day outside. Yesterday's rain is still fresh on the roads and hanging from the leaves, but a well-rested sun is shining bright through the droplets. The light reflects from the damp streets and the glare stings your eyes a little. You'd feel stupid wearing sunglasses on a day like today but you probably need them.

Walk out to driveway and head left down the street. Dad picks up the pace, striding forward with purpose. Speed up slightly to keep up, even though you feel it in your legs. The blood starts pumping and you can feel the impact of the concrete with each step, rattling through your stiff knees and landing in your hips.

As you carry on down the road, your muscles start to loosen and you find your stride. The fresh air fills your lungs and your chest expands. Your back starts loosening up and you feel a lot lighter.

Dad is marching along beside you, arms swinging slightly. Each step is uniform and he moves at a consistent pace. No time to stop and look around, just get from A to B, get the body moving. But he seems like he's loosening up a bit too, his shoulders are dropping and the deep lines on his forehead have softened slightly.

You walk for twenty minutes, eventually leaving the houses behind and getting lost in the trees around the park. Not being able to see anything outside of the green feels relaxing. It's just

271

like your protective bubble in front of the TV, turned away from the responsibilities looming in the distance.

Feel a slight ache in your legs as you start to get tired now. Your breath is getting quicker and a few beads of sweat start winding their way down your forehead. You try to hide it but you're struggling to get enough air in. Eventually, dad notices you pulling in huge breaths and sees your face turning red.

"Alright?"
"Just need a breather."

There's an old bench nearby, tucked away in a small pocket between the trees. You both sit down and you hunch over, trying to get your breath back again.

Sunlight creeps through the canopy and lights up the pollen and dust, floating through the air. The whole place has a warm green glow to it. The smell of the fallen leaves breaking down into the dirt fills your senses as you catch your breath. Turn to see dad watching you.

"Sorry, I'm just struggling a bit."

He puts a hand on your shoulder and nods his head slowly, trying to force a smile.

"We're all struggling a bit. We'll be alright though."

He squeezes your shoulder and pats you on the back before turning to look out over the park. The sweat dries on your forehead and you start cooling down. When you feel ready to get moving again, you stand up and stretch your back out a bit. Dad gets up and brushes his trousers off.

"Shall we head home and get something to eat? I'm starving."

You'd forgotten how hungry you were until he mentioned it, but it comes on strong as soon as he does. Agree and turn back towards home. On the way, you notice him glancing over at you, adjusting his speed so you can keep up.

He looks different somehow. The organised, put together man that doesn't let anything knock him off course has faded away and you see the real person underneath. You spent so long wondering what the secret is, how everybody manages to plan every second of their life and shoulder all their responsibilities, and how that's supposed to make them happy.

But walking back home with him, you wonder whether there is a secret at all. The truth is, there's no formula for keeping everything together because nobody really is. We're all just falling from one day to the next, dealing with whatever comes our way. There are no rules, it's just one foot in front of the other.

You arrive home as the sun disappears and the dark sets in. The onset of night-time makes you even hungrier. You get in and throw your coat off. Dad suggests a takeaway, so you start going through the list, trying to decide what to have.

Chinese? Neither of you really fancy it. What about Indian? It's a bit heavy. Chippy? It doesn't really travel well- the chips and batter will be soggy by the time it arrives.

You give up on your phone, maybe too much choice is making it impossible to land on a decision. Dad suggests doing things the old-fashioned way, so he delves into the messy drawer in the kitchen and pulls out a bunch of crumpled menus.

Half of the places are closed down or turned into something else. The rest don't interest either of you, so you're stuck again.

You suggest making something, so you both rummage through the cupboards looking for something quick and easy. But everything you come across requires too much effort or it doesn't quite satisfy the incredibly vague, but also very specific craving you both have. There is something particular but neither of you have a clue what it is.

You can see dad is getting frustrated. He's not used to living such a chaotic life. Normally, everything is planned in advance and he knows what he's having for dinner already. This is as close as he gets to living on the edge and the lack of control doesn't sit well with him.

He goes into the fridge for one more look. He sticks his head inside and pauses for a second, before leaning out and slowly turning to you. He gives you a very rare grin.

"There's cake in the fridge, and a couple of cans of Coke to wash it down with."

Later that night, mum comes in to find the dark living room illuminated by the TV. You and dad both lay asleep on the sofa, cake crumbs littered over your chests. She smiles and switches the TV off.

LIFE IS A DRINK

Recently I've been thinking about how I wish life had been described to me. I wish someone had told me that it's like being tiny and falling into a glass full of liquids of different viscosities. Sometimes you'll fall through it like water, and it'll be refreshing and cool and it'll race by you and you'll think this ought to be harder.

Then suddenly you hit something gooey, like oil, and it sticks to your skin and pulls your arm hairs together and you don't know whether this is forever or if resistance will be thin again. It's then that you realise you can see people ahead that are falling quicker than you and it's too easy to blame yourself for not being slicker. Just remember you won't fail, you're just in a thicker section of the cocktail.

Once you get used to seeing people falling at different velocities and the feeling of each layer's viscosity you might even see the end. The bottom of the glass. It's okay if some days it seems appealing or if reaching it sends you reeling. The end changes shape, warps and can appear closer, but remember it's usually an illusion. It just depends on how the light bends in this layer of the solution.

The upshot of this life drink is it's a lot to take but you'll never taste anything quite as sweet. The most important thing is to enjoy it, drink it in and serve it neat.

Here we go again. Do you remember the first time? Before we went in it was a mess of worries in our head. Everybody's heard stories about how the drugs affect you. They all want to know whether they'll be strong enough to make it through. We were just the same, sitting in this same cramped waiting room, running over the same horror stories again and again, terrified of what would happen on the other side of that door.

Looking around the room, it's easy to spot the first timers from the ones that are here for yet another round.

The veterans look bored, their days of being nervous are over. They've been there, done that, and they don't even get a t-shirt. They know exactly what to expect and they know that no matter how many times they've been through it before, they won't be able to prepare themselves. No amount of pre-planning and experience can prevent the toll that the drugs take on their body.

We know this all too well. The concoction rips through our veins and spreads through the body, slowly draining our energy and killing our immune system, leaving us weak and exhausted. But there's no use fighting it, we know it's going to happen, so we just have to let ourselves sink through it until we come out the other side.

That's the difference between the veterans and the first timers. They look scared. They're not relaxed like the rest of us, waiting patiently for our turn. Their eyes are fixed on the ground as they try to drag themselves away somewhere, hide inside their heads and escape the crushing fear for just a moment. What they don't realise is that the more you fight it, the bigger it gets.

Eventually, after a while of waiting and staring at the faded yellowy walls, they call our name. Get up, no need to rush, just go through the motions. They lead us through the double doors and into a small examination room.

Do you remember how we felt the first time we pushed through those doors? Now, it's second nature, we just want it over with. We sit down at the desk opposite the friendly nurse with his clipboard. Why do we have to go through the same questions every time? The answers haven't changed since the first visit.

Once the questions are finished, he brings out the sleeve and wraps it around our arm. There is a background hum as it inflates and squeezes just a little too tight. He notes down our blood pressure and then gestures towards the scales. Step on, wait for him to write down the number, step off again. Stand still while he measures our height, listen for the beep of the thermometer. We know this procedure off by heart now.

That's what a lot of life is really, procedure. Just rolling on, doing mostly the same things every day. That used to be terrifying.

In the past, we were always fixated on this idea of having a grand purpose. Unless we could find our calling and do something truly great, how could we ever be happy? We thought that the endless repetition of life would slowly crush us, but that's because we were looking in all the wrong places.

That fear of a life wasted weighed on us and dragged us into the darkest of places. It's like we'd been dropped into the cocktail of life with all its layers and we were stuck in a thick, oily mass. We slowed to a grinding halt as we watched everybody around us propel themselves forward with purpose. It was difficult to see things clearly when we only saw ourselves in the mirror of other people.

But this whole thing showed us that the procedure of life isn't important, and it's nothing to be feared. Sure, we still want to find our own way and do something exciting with our time here. After all you never know when life will take a sharp left turn towards a cliff edge.

That doesn't mean we should run from the mundane parts of life, though. It's in those ordinary moments that we find the extraordinary joys. How many family dinners or car rides from the train station did we take for granted? When we first got diagnosed and the family rallied around us, suddenly, the boring bits felt so important to us.

The nurse finishes his examination and takes us through to the treatment room. Beds lined up with the bags waiting. A cocktail of harsh chemicals ready to wash the colour from our body and leave us a black and white tracing of a person. A nurse waits patiently while we sink into the chair and lean back, presenting an arm. She wipes the vein with an alcohol wipe. The cooling sensation makes us shiver slightly as she presses the needle in our skin. It's an odd sensation, but it's barely noticeable anymore. Then the thick liquid starts flowing.

Sitting here, watching the bag slowly empty, we're a million miles from the person we were a few years ago, back when we thought that the world was conspiring against us, our days and nights latching on to every bad thought.

Don't worry, I'm not blaming us, it's a mistake most people make. We were like those people sitting out there, waiting to come in here for the first time. Now, we know that you've just got to lay back and let it flow through you, and deal with whatever comes after.

But they're inside their own heads, trying to make sense of it. They spend hours researching the potential side effects and reading up on other people's experiences. They fill their heads with a mess of information, all of it useless.

278

What is that they say about quicksand? You're not supposed to try to climb out, you're supposed to stand still and just let it happen. Eventually, once you stop fighting it, you stop sinking and it's easy to climb out and keep walking.

There was a time when we kicked back and tried to fight instead of letting ourselves sink. In a moment like this, when we feel our body starting to get weaker and we know it's only going to get worse, it's easy to imagine that this is all there is.

The liquid in the bag slowly fills us up and weighs us down until we stop moving. But fixating on the bad days only makes you blind to the good ones.

Remember standing on stage, reading our poetry out loud for the first time? That rush of adrenaline was born partly from fear, from the worry that everybody would think it was shit and we'd be a laughing stock. But even though it was so far outside of our comfort zone, it somehow felt safe. It was like returning home after getting caught in the rain. That relief when you finally find respite from the grey skies and the cold that rattles you to the core. Stepping down from the stage, we breathed a sigh of relief because it felt like the oil was being washed away and we were moving into clear waters.

Thinking about it, that's why we decided to print out those poems and put them together in the right order. We're telling a story, a cautionary tale to help other people that find themselves lost.

If we knew back then what was coming, we never would have wasted so much time. We would have grabbed hold of life and drank it all in, the good and the bad. We can't go back now, but at least we can tell our story and stop other people from making the same mistakes.

Look at this place. You'd think they could make it a bit

nicer. We've got to sit here, watching as the bag slowly empties
into our arm and leaves us hollow, the least they could do is
give it a fresh coat of paint.

It doesn't really matter. We'll be home soon, surrounded by

family and warm memories. Just a little while longer and we'll
be done, so no need to complain about it.

It really felt like we had some momentum before we hit the
brick wall. We were doing things our own way, even when
everybody around us thought it was the wrong way. Things
finally seemed like they were on the right track and we were
close to figuring out the secret to a happy and fulfilled life.

Then, one trip to the hospital and the whole world collapsed
around us. Everything was turned upside down and we were
thrown into a bubble. An endless cycle of treatments and
sitting around at home while life went on outside.

Plenty of people would call it unfair. They'd wonder how it

could possibly make sense that after finally dragging ourselves
out of the dark and getting back on our feet, something like
this could happen to us. Is it shit luck, or maybe a malicious

God playing a sick game? It's neither, it's just life.

Nearly done now. The last few drops wind their way down
the tube and into our arm. The nurse sees that the bag is
empty and comes over. She carefully removes the needle. I

wonder if we'll ever get used to the sensation of it sliding out

and seeing the tiny hole it leaves behind.

She puts the needle to one side and quickly patches the hole

with a clump of cotton wool. Push it down to stop the bleeding.

This is the worst part, the waiting to go home. Don't worry, it's

ok to be annoyed about it. This is just one of those bad days that comes in between the good ones. There's no sense pretending that it isn't.

Just don't will the bad days to disappear- it only leads to more of them. When you're constantly trying to force yourself to be content and happy every single day, you only kick yourself when you aren't.

We used to be like that, always searching for the one thing that would turn life into a rollercoaster of excitement without a dull day in sight. There's a lot of dull days now. Plenty of days spent in hospitals or sitting at home, searching for the energy to get up and do something. But there's a lot of good days too, and the difficult times put a mirror up to the memories that should be savoured.

That's the thing, you can't pick and choose. People love to think that they're the centre of everything and if they can grab hold of life and pin it down, they can mould it in whatever way they want. Everybody's always trying to pick out the bad bits like a kid with a plate full of vegetables.

That's how life is sold to us. Work hard, make the right decisions and it'll all be fine. Do something you love and you'll never work a day in your life, and once you're on the right track, it's all plain sailing. No bad days in sight.

We only need to look in the mirror for proof that it doesn't work that way. Life does what it wants to us and that's fine. We don't have much say in what happens to us, only how we react to it. Just take it as it comes and enjoy the ride.

After a while of sitting, we're taken in to speak to the nurse again. It's the usual stuff, how to manage the side effects, what we can and can't take, drink plenty of water to flush it all out. We know it all by now, just nod along and say thank you, we'll be out of here soon.

The walk through the hospital is always longer on the way back. Our legs are stiff from sitting down for so long and the drugs are starting to sap at the energy we have.

Each step thuds into the concrete floor and the impact shoots through our entire body. The nurse paces herself beside us as we drag ourselves down long hallways, the end moving towards us an inch at a time.

Every time we round a corner we're faced with another daunting corridor with a barely visible end. A few quiet bodies in gowns shuffle past as we march on. The buzz of the fluorescent light vibrates through us as we scrunch our eyes and try to block it out.

But we keep pushing on, winding through the corridors into the lift. You and the nurse stand in silence as it slowly creeps down, stopping at every floor along the way.

It feels like hours since we got up from that chair and started the journey out of this place. Grim faces get in and out of the lift. Nervous families are glad of the few moments of silence as they ride down. Bored regulars, back for yet another treatment, stare into the corner, trying to find somewhere else in their heads.

Finally, the lift reaches the bottom floor, and the doors ping open. As they slide back, the first bit of light starts breaking through. A few distant flashes of sunlight creep down the corridors towards the heart of the hospital. The heavy weight on our chest starts lifting a little. The hardest part is over.

It's noisier down here. The bustle of names being called, and people being directed this way and that is refreshing. Everybody moves with more urgency than they did upstairs.

We move left and right, dodging around people and heading towards the outside. Turn a corner to a large wall of windows, the sunlight washing over people hurrying up and down the corridor. The claustrophobic atmosphere is lifting and we're starting to pick up the pace. Breathe deeply and feel the hint of fresh air, bleeding in from the outside.

One final corner and there it is, the front door. The tightness in our legs starts melting away and our shoulders drop.

One foot in front of the other. That's the secret really, that's the thing we should have been taught about life years ago. It's one foot in front of the other, it's just the surroundings that change. There's no secret formula for avoiding the bad days, and we shouldn't be trying to either.

When we run from the difficult days, we convince ourselves that they're forever. If we let them catch up with us, they'll consume us and drag us down into the dirt. That's not how it works, though.

Adversity slows us down and we look around at everybody else, moving through life with ease, and it's easy to feel bad. But when we remember that we'll soon be moving again, once we pass through this slow patch, it's easier to hold on. Just focus on the small wins and find the things that make us lucky, even when everything else seems hopeless.

Don't regret the bad days either, cherish them. They're all part of the cocktail, they're central to the experience. They only highlight the things you should be grateful for and show you where your priorities should be. We lost sight of that for a while but when the worst thing in the world happened to us, it gave us the clarity that we needed.

Life isn't always joy and despair either, most of the time it's just a middle ground. The mundane days are littered with the small moments that make life the varied, beautiful, unpredictable mess that it is.

We finally make it to the front door and look out over the car park. The doors slide back and the wind hits us. The refreshing cold washes away the slow feeling. Take a deep breath and feel it fill your lungs. Smell the slight hint of petrol mixed with the muddy leaves gathered in the corner of the pavement by the wind. Listen to the gentle rumble of cars creeping along, looking for a space.

Wave to our mum and dad, waiting to pick us up. The nurse pats us on the shoulder and watches us cross the car park.

It's a relief to leave and get in the car back home. The warmth of the air conditioning fills our cheeks as soon as we get in and shut the door. The warm smiles and the cramped back seat feel safe and comfortable. For a few moments, everything disappears into the background and we forget about the endless chemo sessions and the toll it's taking on us.

Look back at the hospital as dad pulls away and creeps into the long line of traffic. It won't be long until we're back here again, but we've got some time before that. We can go home, spend time with the family, do the important things. While we're waiting to find out how this ends, we can put all those poems together and release them to the world. It's too late to get back the time that we lost but our mistakes can serve as a warning to others.

When we first started writing our thoughts down it was just for us. It was a way to organise the mess and try to make sense of our own head. We never thought that we would end up sharing them with the world. But now, it's clear that we need to. That's their purpose and if we keep hold of them, they aren't helping anybody.

That's what we need to focus on now, putting it all together and setting them free. Beyond that, we just need to keep getting up and getting on with it.

Some days will be better than others. Some are going to be hard. Just keep moving forward and remember, life is a lot to take, but you'll never taste anything quite as sweet. The most important thing is to enjoy it, drink it in, and serve it neat.

The End

Printed in Great Britain
by Amazon

26169035R00165